THE JOBS REVOLUTION

Changing How America Works

Steve Gunderson, Roberts Jones, Kathryn Scanland

Copyright © 2005 by Copywriters Incorporated.

All rights reserved under International and Pan-American Copyright Conventions.

Published in the United States of America by Copywriters Incorporated, a division of The Greystone Group, Inc.

Library of Congress Cataloging-in-Publication Data

Steve Gunderson, Roberts Jones and Kathryn Scanland
THE JOBS REVOLUTION: Changing How America Works

p. cm.
Includes index.

ISBN 0-9749952-1-5
1. Employment   2. Public Policy   3. Workforce   4. Global Economy

Printed in the United States of America.

Second Edition

Book Design by Rolf M. Smith, Progressive AE
Cover Design By Stephen J. Waudby, Creative Cube Studio

www.jobsrevolution.com

"Most of us are about as eager to change as we were to be born, and go through our changes in a similar state of shock."

James Baldwin

"What we have before us are some breathtaking opportunities disguised as insoluble problems."

John Gardner

Dedication

To the nation's professionals
engaged in preparing our future workforce.

Acknowledgements

A year ago the first edition of ***The Jobs Revolution*** appeared. We believed then that people engaged in the noble cause of preparing our future workforce wanted a simple, concise summary of the changing American workforce and workplace. We thank them for confirming our judgment.

As it turned out, the first edition went places we'd not imagined. Policymakers like Senator Mike Enzi of Wyoming – the Chairman of the Senate's Committee on Health, Education, Labor and Pensions – found the book a useful tool. It was a guide for young adults seeking a path for their professional career and a starting point for strategic planning by educators and economic development specialists. Journalists and community leaders said it was a "wakeup call" for America's future.

Our first printing sold out. But a second edition is needed because, while basic concepts articulated in the first edition remain the same, statistics reporting the stories are changing dramatically. Some changes are relatively trivial (we spoke of 50 million web sites last year; it's 57 million today). Other changes in demographic information are more critical. We've reviewed each statistic in the book, updating what we could and confirming accuracy throughout.

In addition to those who helped craft our first edition, we want to pay a special thanks to Tori Gorman, Patty Edmonds and Rick Corcoran for their work. They have become partners in this noble journey, giving us new data, new insights and new accuracy.

Personal experiences, analyses and perspectives are gifts we've received from thousands of people across the nation who have listened to our presentations and shared their insights with us. We are better because you have made us more thoughtful.

As we continue this journey, we again thank our colleagues at The Greystone Group, Inc., and friends old and new across the nation. If we stay committed to change built on real evidence, shaped to real outcomes, we can – together – make a real difference.

Steve Gunderson
Roberts Jones
Kathryn Scanland

Contents

Chapter 1	Why Daddy Didn't Work Today	1
Chapter 2	A Revolutionary Nation	9
Chapter 3	America in the World	17
Chapter 4	Shortage of Workers, Shortage of Skills	27
Chapter 5	New Faces in the Workplace	33
Chapter 6	Looking for a Job?	43
Chapter 7	Taking Jobs to Market	51
Chapter 8	Education for Employment	59
Chapter 9	The Long View: Revolution in Context	67
Chapter 10	What's a Community to Do?	73
Chapter 11	In Need of a Champion	83
Chapter 12	Training Chauffeurs	95

Chapter One

Why Daddy Didn't Work Today

Applebee's restaurant had arrived in Greenville, Michigan, less than a year earlier. Down the road stood a charming bed-and-breakfast, once home to the Gibson family that gave generations of American housewives their refrigerators, still wearing its holiday wreaths when the news broke on Friday, January 16, 2004.

"WAGE GAP DOOMS PLANT" roared headlines in The Grand Rapids Press, the region's largest daily. The doomed plant was Greenville's century-old Gibson facility now owned by Electrolux Home Products North America, the U.S.-based arm of a Swedish ownership group. Greenville operations will close in 2005 when Electrolux's new plant opens in Juarez, Mexico.

Days later Greenville's Daily News carried an obituary of an editorial: "November 2005 will mark the end of 2,781 jobs at the Greenville plant and 500 more directly related to Electrolux being here.... Tis truly a sad day."

The loss of 3,281 jobs is staggering in a town of 7,935. Equally staggering are cost comparisons between U.S.-based and Mexico-based manufacturing. Electrolux CEO Hans Straberg told financial analysts that he could shut his Greenville operations for $154 million and save $81 million a year

The numbers spell a story of massive savings for Electrolux, lower costs for refrigerator buyers, higher profits for stockholders and heartbreaking losses for the people of Greenville, Michigan.

1

operating in Mexico. He'd recoup his closing costs in less than two years. Thereafter, $81 million in annual savings would help Electrolux compete with lower-cost competitors (refrigerator prices fell 16 percent between 1998 and 2002) and with higher profits.

Unions in Greenville offered $32 million in annual wage concessions (reportedly, a third of some workers' income). State and local authorities offered another $20 million in tax relief and aid. But hourly wages in Greenville in 2004, including benefits, averaged $22.99. South of the border, they averaged $3.65. Mexican tax rates are one-fourth those in the U.S. The numbers spell a story of massive savings for Electrolux, lower costs for refrigerator buyers, higher profits for stockholders and heartbreaking losses for the people of Greenville, Michigan.

More people of wider age-ranges and more varied educational and economic status are able to access more information, more quickly, at lower costs and greater ease than at any time in human history.

The same day Greenville's editor, among others, took to bashing Mexico, NAFTA and all the usual suspects (January 19, 2004), TIME Magazine published an interview with Mexico's President Vicente Fox. Fox's chief concern? China, to which 100,000-200,000 Mexican jobs had recently migrated. It was the problem Fox had discussed in Sweden with Electrolux CEO Straberg three months earlier.

Greenville's citizens blamed Mexico while Mexico's president pointed his finger at China. Their complaints were roughly the same. As it turns out, in Jaurez, Mexico, as in Greenville, Michigan, children wonder why daddy didn't work today, and fathers as well as mothers wonder where their jobs will come from tomorrow.

Gregg Easterbrook notes how radically jobs have changed in his insightful book, *The Progress Paradox*. "When you call or e-mail Amazon.com, the friendly voice or politely typed reply comes not from Seattle but Bangalore, India, where the company's customer service department is now located." The Call Center Association of India, a national trade group, now boasts two million Indians earning "their livings by answering 800 numbers for American and European firms."[1]

Americans clamor for ever-lower taxes and smaller government bureaucracies, but the State of New Jersey wasn't ready for what Easterbrook reported:

> If you phone the New Jersey state welfare agency to ask about your benefits, your call is taken by a representative sitting in India and speaking by satellite link. The India-based call-taker costs New Jersey about three dollars per hour in wages and benefits, versus the fifteen dollars an hour the state would pay to put a welfare recipient to work answering calls about welfare.[2]

When New Jersey's elected authorities discovered that they were managing costs through a strategy Easterbrook was sharing with America, they adopted legislation ending this practice.

It's possible to legislate how the State government employs its workforce. But it is not possible to legislate prices on all products sold in America. Our national affection for rock-bottom pricing has enabled the American giant, Wal-Mart, to become the largest corporation on the face of the globe. It's an all-American firm buying from the global marketplace, contributing daily to the export of American jobs because Americans like low prices.

What's happening in Greenville and Juarez is actually happening around the globe. Jobs we believed would always be available, probably even plentiful, are disappearing. Most jobs have not fled across any border; they've simply dissolved through efficiencies in process engineering, technology and corporate strategy ("productivity gains"). Outsourcing actually accounts for less than 10 percent of the American jobs lost in the last three years. Projections by Forrester Research of up to 3.4 million jobs outsourced by 2015 remains less than 3 percent of total U.S. employment.[3] But these are numbers, not news stories. And jobs heading across the border make news. One day our daddy carries a lunch bucket to the factory; the next he sits at home watching Oprah because daddy isn't qualified for new jobs becoming available.

The 3,281 folk facing unemployment in Greenville are not comforted that, on average, we have better healthcare, longer lives, fewer accidents, more education, higher per capita income and shorter work weeks than our grandparents could have imagined. In 2001, more of us were working than ever before. Optimism should abound. But those who've lost their jobs are not optimistic; they're frightened, angry, hurt. Jobs are how we put bread on the table and a sense of worth in our souls. Lose our jobs and we lose more than a paycheck.

Progress is always good news. Our ancestors watched for the once-a-year arrival of Sears & Roebuck's catalog so they could align their dreams with pencil sketches of new-fangled inventions. Their great-grandchildren cruise the Internet at roughly the speed of light spending dollars annually in a number great-grandfather would not have known: "billions." Money invested to build, play and work along this information superhighway fueled the economic boom of the 1990s. Even now, more people of wider age-ranges and more varied educational and economic status are able to access more information, more quickly, at lower costs and with greater ease than at any time in human history.

What's troubled isn't so much the American economy as the workforce inside that economy. For those with requisite education and skills, jobs are mostly secure and times are mostly good. For those who lack the flexibility given by education and skills, employment is uncertain and it's a worrisome world. Especially those who stopped their education during or after high school now fear they'll soon be paraphrasing songs from the musical South Pacific, "What ain't we got? We ain't got jobs!"

If I am unemployed, the jobs revolution doesn't seem like progress. It seems like a very, very bad idea.

The rhetoric accompanying the jobs revolution is rich in accusation and blame but poor in analysis and candor. It's easy to point to the carnage that accompanies plant closings and to play to the fear of the unknown. We all feel something sinister when a distant corporate office can turn grown men from satisfying labor to thoughts of suicide. But blame does not produce reliable answers or employ the unemployed.

Making political hay out of workforce troubles serves no good purpose. When people who know better talk of outsourcing jobs to India and China, and blame NAFTA for it, they are playing games. America doesn't have broad, free-trade agreements with India or China, so NAFTA – or some variation on it – is not to blame. Something else is at work here, something that begs to be understood, not blamed.

America doesn't have broad, free-trade agreements with India or China, so NAFTA – or some variation on it – is not to blame. Something else is at work here, something that begs to be understood, not blamed.

Here's a simple fact: Between 1993 and 2003 factory productivity in the U.S. increased some 47 percent.[4] This means that factories made 47 percent more stuff using the same number of employees. When productivity rockets up at this rate, factory jobs will disappear no matter what. We can scream "freeze" to trade, but jobs will still evaporate. No political candidate rails against productivity gains because we all like what these gains bring us: better healthcare and communication, lower prices for comparable goods, greater educational opportunity, a broader array of affordable choices, more high-tech and white-collar jobs and a continually rising standard of living. We merely don't want to pay the cost of these gains in unemployment, especially my unemployment.

If we can get beyond the rhetoric we'll discover that unemployment is not the necessary cost of the jobs revolution. We need less rhetoric and a hefty, candid dose of reality. Then we can shape policies that support Americans suffering in this revolution, programs that block injury in the future, and investments – both public and private – that are critical to our national interest.

The reality of life and labor in the 21st Century is that we'll never go back. We'll never return to days before satellites hovered over the globe and the Internet wove us together. We need to go forward, guided by a plan that reflects a realistic understanding of what's happening and that promotes a new set of American priorities.

The plan will marry education and employment. In the old, pre-revolutionary model, we went to school for a dozen or more years and then we went to work. After this revolution we'll need to keep learning to keep working. Education and re-education will be the dominant strategy by which we land and hold our jobs.

The plan will demand policies measured to global realities and American need. We can't build a wall around the nation and escape the world marketplace – and we don't need to. America is capable of preparing, placing and compensating the most gifted and diverse workforce in the history of the world. But we need, quickly and thoroughly, to reshuffle our local, regional and national policies.

Public and private investment, at amounts within our reach, can make the plan work. How we invest the money will be critical. We need to invest in keeping people employable and stop defining workforce investment as a social benefit in a second-chance system. Workforce development is economic development and it yields a fabulous ROI ("return on investment").

As Greenville recovers from its collective shock, it will stop playing the blame game. The city will learn what this book reports. A revolution is underway. Communities reeling from hard news, companies needing a gifted workforce, parents hungering for reliable jobs, policy makers setting a course into the future – all of us need to act now.

It's not yet too late. But Will Rogers had it right: "Even if you're on the right track, you'll get run over if you just sit there."

Chapter Two

A Revolutionary Nation

Rev-o-lu-tion: noun; 1) revolving, single complete orbit or rotation; 2) complete change of method or conditions, 3) substitution of a new system of government, esp. by force, 4) change, reorganization, transformation, upheaval.[5]

Throughout history Americans have managed change, usually with reluctance or resignation. We prefer time to plan because orderly change is less traumatic. Even our founding fathers didn't start with a revolution in mind. They wanted a return to stable relations with Great Britain. That didn't happen and they, too, managed.

We've been helped by the fact that some revolutions came slowly enough to allow the next generation to manage the change, so dad kept plowing with horses while sons climbed onto tractors. Changes of this type are now remembered as "progress." But progress was paid for with emotional, economic and sometimes physical pain.

The word "revolution" in this book's title is an instructive, not a rhetorical, term. What's happening is best understood – perhaps *only* understood – as a revolution. Massive changes are occurring too quickly for the baby-boom generation to wait for the next generation to take it on.

> *The word "revolution" in this book's title is an instructive, not a rhetorical, term. What's happening is best understood – perhaps only understood – as a revolution.*

We're already experiencing the most profound *rotation* of workers ever, in any country, at any time. It cuts through workplaces and classrooms, family finances and our individual senses of self-worth. Even though it is an *upheaval*, its arrival was predictable for those willing to see it coming.

America is a revolutionary nation. We were born in the American Revolution, moved West in the Agricultural Revolution, built our cities during the Industrial Revolution and assumed global leadership in the Information Revolution.

Consider the American Revolution. The British government wanted more control over the colonies' political activities and commerce. Over a three-year period beginning in 1764 the crown hammered the colonies with the Sugar Act, Currency Act, Stamp Act, Customs Collecting Act and Tea Act progressively tightening King George's grip on his American territory. When the American colonists assembled for their first Continental Congress (September 1774) what they had in mind was going back to where they'd been. Their resolutions called for rights but never for revolution.

Up to three hundred hours of labor were required to produce 100 bushels of wheat on a five-acre plot around 1830. By 1850 farms had seen such a revolution in efficiency that only 75-to-90 hours of labor were need to yield the same 100 bushels of corn – and this on half the acreage (2.5 acres) needed in 1830.

In April of 1775 British troops marched towards Lexington, Massachusetts to gain control over a military arsenal, evoking the famous ride of Paul Revere. A month later the Continental Congress assembled for a second time with most delegates still wanting a "recovery," a peaceful resolution of disputes with British authorities. Even after the Declaration of Independence separated the colonies from Britain, most American soldiers – farmers drafted by their colonial governments – were more worried about jobs than war. When their terms of enlistment were over, the vast majority simply walked home to get back to work regardless of the military needs on the battlefield.

Citizens of the new American nation were not highly educated. Churches and taverns offered what news and commentary most people received. Organized learning – America's first public school had been founded a century-and-a-half earlier in Boston – focused primarily on literacy and arithmetic.[6] The most elite colonists had college training but most boys learned skills needed in manhood by working next to fathers and uncles. Girls were tutored in the kitchen and nursery for a life of homemaking. Learning and work were so intertwined that it was unclear where a lesson ended and a job began.

Then came the Agricultural Revolution. By 1790 the American population had grown to just under four million people, 90 percent of them farmers. As immigrants squeezed onto the eastern seaboard, the nation expanded westward with the government providing land surveys and sales in minimum plots of at least 640 acres.

America was Europe's farm. Blacksmiths partnered with farmers to produce equipment unheard of in other times and places. Each cotton gin (1793) displaced dozens of farm laborers. The cast-iron plow built by blacksmiths in 1797 was converted, in 1834, to a steel-bladed classic produced in mass volume by Leonard Andrus and John Deere, men who understood the buying market in a nation of farmers.

Productivity gains were staggering. Up to three hundred hours of labor were required to produce 100 bushels of wheat on a five-acre plot around 1830. By 1850 farms had seen such a revolution in efficiency that only 75 to 90 hours of labor were needed to yield the same 100 bushels of corn – and this on half the acreage (2.5 acres) needed in 1830.

Farmers and merchants were buoyed by optimism. Slavery shadowed the American experience, but for free men a life of reward and satisfaction could be realized by all through honest and hard work.[7] Land was cheap. An "employee" was typically an apprentice who, through diligent labor, would become an owner. So work-based was most education that school enrollments – despite regular efforts at local and federal levels to increase it – remained dismally low, around 50 percent for those aged 5-19 in 1900.[8]

Throughout the Agricultural Revolution American colleges and universities were mostly under-funded and desperate for students. Some paid students to attend. Well into the late 1800s Harvard's four-year bachelor's degree, even its famed master's degree, were mostly a prize for attendance. Students who paid an annual fee enabled faculty to eat. Their reward was the coveted sheepskin too pricey for most Americans.[9]

America's revolutions have been international revolutions. The Declaration of Independence borrowed French philosophy and politics. The Agricultural Revolution was spurred by international trade. And the American Industrial Revolution was no different. England, stuffed with too many workers through the 1700s and 1800s, used machinery mostly to improve quality; mechanization was all about precision, not productivity. But America was sparsely populated. The need on this side of the Atlantic was for increased efficiency and production.[10] Thus, machines were created to improve the output, not the precision, of the American laborer. In 1807 America had 15 cotton mills operating a total of

By 1990 farmers, once 90 percent of the workforce, comprised 2.6 percent of the nation's workers. Less than 3 hours of farm labor could produce 100 bushels of corn.

8,000 spindles. In less than ten years (by 1815) 500,000 spindles were operating under the guide of 76,000 employees.[11] Change came overnight and was all about productivity.

It required five generations for the American farm to give way to the factory. Mass production needed workers, not owners. Divisions of labor led to the specialist task worker who helped make a product but didn't finish it. Since each worker added only a portion to a finished product, wages were no longer based on "how many products I finished" but on "how long I worked on the line."

By the dawn of World War Two public education had become the assumed course for American children to follow to adulthood. Parents and job requirements combined to drive up enrollment rates from 51 percent in 1900 to 75 percent in 1940. Formal education, once the province of the elite, had been transformed into learning units that mostly equipped women for home and men for trades. Agricultural colleges helped keep American farms the envy of the globe.

After revolutions of independence, agriculture and industry came information. The seeds of this revolution were planted in 1947 in the Bell Laboratories with the invention of the transistor. Thereafter, the transistor gave birth to memory chips (1958); chips begat micro-processors; micro-processors begat calculators and word processors; calculators and word processors begat the personal computer and the "information age" had dawned. The 1971 chip contained 2,300 transistors; one released in 2000 contained 42 million transistors.[12] The revolution that dawned 30 years ago is already at high noon. It came fast. Knowledge once limited to those haunting graduate school libraries is now at the disposal of eight-year-olds playing on the Internet.

Information technology and the Internet now account for one-third of America's economic growth, impact every sector of our workforce, are revamping every classroom at all levels – the personal computer *is* the classroom for on-line and distance learning – and in 2000 produced jobs paying almost 80 percent above the private-sector average.[13]

And so we have endured our revolutions. By 1990 farmers, once 90 percent of the U.S. workforce, comprised 2.6 percent of the nation's workers. Less than 3 hours of farm labor could produce 100 bushels of corn. The farm's fax machine was soon joined by personal computers connected, wireless, to resources and markets around the globe.

Following World War Two America's public schools saw enrollment rates approaching 90 percent for 5-19 year olds. Higher education was flooded with military veterans and others who'd postponed college education due to the Depression.[14]

Through the 1960s, girls in high school learned to type and boys learned basic trades in "shop." It was a classic mismatch of education and employment. As a result, by 1984 business and industry provided nearly as many courses for adults as did four-year colleges and universities[15] because Americans were not equipped to work in the dawning information age. Those without advanced education saw the doors of opportunity closing to professional and managerial jobs throughout the 1980s.[16]

We will not be going back to recover what earlier generations, and we, once had; the model of a "recovery" is wrong.

The full-scale addition of personal computers, the Internet and the World Wide Web bore down on America's workplace during the 1990s. Those lacking advanced education were challenged to hang onto jobs. Those who couldn't type needed to learn. Male executives struggled for dignity as they scrambled to find "secretaries" who could receive and print e-mail for them. It didn't last. By 2000 men who had once prided themselves on being unable to type were mastering keyboards at an amazing pace.

Information technology has bull-dozed traditional barriers of distance and culture. In the new world, as Peter Drucker insists, "with knowledge becoming the key resource… the educated person now matters."[17] Steve Gunderson cites, as evidence, his nephew Brad Boeckmann's 2003 essay submitted as part of his college application:

> *My Grandfather, Art Gunderson, has in his own quiet way opened my eyes to a new 21st Century world developing before us. As a young man growing up on his family's farm my grandfather obtained the ultimate in educational achievement, a high school degree. Soon after, he joined the United States Navy and left home for the very first time to participate in World War Two. His fear was not going to war but rather going so far away from home. When the war was over, he returned to his hometown of Pleasantville, Wisconsin. There he joined with my great-grandfather to convert an old automotive repair shop started during the Depression into the local car dealership selling Chevrolets.*
>
> *This last week, my same grandfather traveled to Germany with my two uncles to attend a dealer orientation program as they prepare to open a new Audi dealership in the outskirts of Los Angeles. In two generations, my family has moved from a rural repair shop on the side of their farm to ownership of an Audi dealership in the metropolis of Los Angeles. In these same*

> *two generations, we've gone from leaving home only to serve in our nation's armed forces to full participation in the 21st Century global economy.*[18]

The jobs revolution is changing where we work, how we work and who works. We cannot walk home from this revolution to go back to work because our jobs are being replaced at the speed of change. Greasy machines are history; computer screens are everywhere. We will not be going back to recover what earlier generations, and we, once had; the model of a "recovery" is wrong. What we did yesterday ("experience") matters but not as much as what we know how to do tomorrow ("knowledge"). For some, this is the great dawn of opportunity. For others, it is the cause of immeasurable angst.

America's jobs are absolutely and irreversibly planted in the new, global world. While CEOs in Sweden are calculating their moves, new knowledge and new technology in America are producing more jobs than are being moved. The challenge we face is taking workers whose jobs are disappearing and moving them into jobs that are being created. For workers with great knowledge and flexible skills, the challenge can be met.

John Dorrer, Director for Labor Market and Workforce Research, Maine Department of Labor, says the situation is best summarized by "the three A's: awareness, ambiguity and anxiety." We are now, or at least we should be, fully aware of the changes that are taking place, and why they are happening. Our policy makers and others are ambiguous about what to make of it all, so leadership is uncertain. And the consequence is a general anxiety across America.[19]

The only way past the ambiguity and anxiety is increased awareness, and a fourth, urgently needed "A": action.

Chapter Three

America in the World

John Naisbitt, famed author of *MegaTrends*, recently wrote:

> *The transcending economic consideration as we move into the 21st Century is the globalization of the world's economies in the direction of a single market world. In the process, we are experiencing a rich paradox. The global economy is of paramount importance, but no one knows how it works. I think that is the good news. If we don't know how it works, we can't fix it.*[20]

This line of thinking is a hard sell to most Americans and very few leaders have been willing to try selling it. Naisbitt's claim may be true but it isn't popular.

When the economy stumbles, we've been quick to accuse someone of tripping us. Voters take aim at politicians. Politicians take aim at other candidates or the other party. We blame foreign nations, immigrants, international trade agreements and multi-national corporations. Mexico is the villain in Greenville, Michigan. India is the whipping boy in Mexico City. China causes our record-high trade deficits, steals our manufacturing jobs and ignores basic

China understands better than the U.S. that higher education is the platform from which to build a sound economy via a skilled workforce. We do not help ourselves by blaming them for being right.

labor and copyright laws. Some truth wanders through this forest of blame, but it doesn't account for the jobs revolution.

Forrester Research, Inc., forecasts that U.S. companies will send 3.4 million service sector jobs overseas by 2015 – most to India.[21] Most Americans respond to such news with a shrug of resignation ("What can I do?") and a note of confusion ("I don't get it."). If more than 70 percent of China's workforce is rural, how can China be such an economic threat to the United States? And if 400 million people in India – half its population – are illiterate, how can they win our high technology jobs?[22]

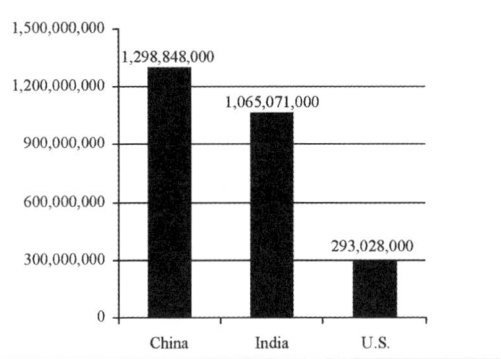

Illustration 1. Population in the World's Three Largest Countries, 2004.

Source: World Almanac, 2005, p. 848.

They can win for two reasons. First, there are more of them than us. India has just over a billion people and China's population exceeds 1.2 billion.[23] They outnumber us four- or five-to-one. If good minds have been spread more or less equally across the human race, then for every good mind in America there are four or five equally good minds at work in India and China. We're being out-thought because we're out-numbered.

Second, they earn less. In 2003, the average Chinese wage was about 3 percent of the wage for similar jobs in the developed world.[24] In India, an IT company could hire an engineer for $12,000, about one-eighth the cost of a comparable engineer in the United States.[25]

Thriving global competition galls most Americans. We frankly don't like the idea that we live in a one-world economy. Something about it seems, well, un-American, making allegations of unfair and unreasonable global competition seem almost patriotic.

Instead of complaining, China and India are competing. Both suffer high percentages of illiterate workers, but their massive populations enable them to produce – or to bring home, after they've graduated from American universities – huge numbers of skilled workers who enable them to lead the competition for global employment.

Evidence of a one-world economy has been abundant for years, but we haven't paid attention. Perhaps we've had a false sense of isolation or even superiority. Approaching the 21st Century we celebrated the defeat of communism in Europe. Terrorism lived mostly across the waters. Our economy was booming. We produced one-fourth of the world's total output with only 4 percent of the world's population. We enjoyed a standard of living reflecting a Gross Domestic Production (GDP) of $37,000 per person—unprecedented in world history and large diverse populations.[26]

Maybe we misjudged the numbing speed with which the global economy would go from prediction to reality. When a decade ago then-Vice Presidential candidate Al Gore promised that the "information super highway" would revolutionize American life, cartoonists had a field day and commentators laughed. Although the authors of

Illustration 2. Current Demographics for Leading Economic Producers per Area.

	China	India	U.S.
Population (millions)*	1,298	1,065	293
Population Growth (percent)*	0.58	1.40	.92
Urbanization (percent)	38.6	28.3	80.1
Population Age 15 or Younger (percent)	24.3	32.7	21.0
Literacy (percent)	86.0	59.5	97.0

Source: World Almanac, 2005. *CIA World Fact Book, 2005.

this book are not recognized as Democrats, we are here to admit that Candidate Gore had it right.

In less than a generation, the world shrank to a fraction of its previous size, whittled down by technology, instant communication, expanded travel and international commerce. We weren't shocked that a Swedish company owned a manufacturing plant in Greenville, Michigan. We probably weren't even shocked when production was moved to Mexico. What shocked us was that it seems to have happened overnight.

We drive our parents to the local hospital for check-ups; we don't notice that their x-rays are relayed electronically to India for reading and analysis. We vacation with a boat trip through London unaware that London's water system is monitored from a control room in India. The world shrank while we tuned-in celebrity trials and "reality TV."

A jobs revolution is upon us and most of us are saying, "Where did this come from?" It came from a global economy we helped produce while most of us weren't looking.

In 2003 the U.S. exported $1 trillion worth of goods and services while we imported things costing some $1.5 trillion.[27] So we have a trade deficit. But the deficit is a fly in the necessary ointment of trade, because trade accounts for nearly $2 *trillion* surging through our national, regional and local American economies. About 87 percent of what we produce and sell stays within U.S. borders, typical of nations around the globe who, on average, export about 12 percent of their goods and services.

The size of the global economy is massive but the jobs revolution has more to do with the *speed* of this growth than its *size*. In 1962, when today's older workers began entering the workforce, America exported $27 billion in goods and services. By 2003 the comparable number was $1 trillion, a 3,700 percent increase. Workers born after World War Two, weaned on "Father Knows Best" and comforted by "The Mickey Mouse Club," were in fact living through a revolution that no one was discussing.

Americans may find the jobs revolution painful but the global economy itself is, mostly, our friend. During the late 1990s export expansion accounted for 25 percent of our domestic economic growth and almost 20 million new jobs. Average annual incomes in the U.S. are nearly 40 percent higher than those of the 650 million people living in other high-income countries.[28] Without the global economy we would suffer untold economic woe and unimaginable unemployment.

The U.S. stake in the global economy will continue to expand through at least the year 2010 (see *Illustration 3*). As our stake grows, the jobs revolution will heat up. As many as 3.3 million high-tech jobs may leave the U.S. in the next decade. This is a large number, but it's also just 2 percent of our jobs, small comfort to the unemployed woman whose job just relocated to Delhi but critical math for those who worry about policy.

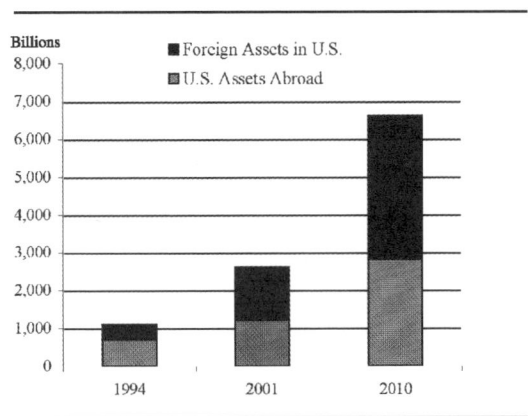

Illustration 3. U.S. Investment Abroad and Foreign Investment in U.S., 1994, 2001 and projected 2010.

Source: Employment Policy Foundation analysis of Bureau of Economic Analysis data, 2003.

The currency of the global economy is knowledge: what we know, not what we have or have done. America remains the economic and military power of the world. But the workplace in California or China, Iowa or India, now recognizes individuals with knowledge and skills more than workers with seniority. The key is not just knowledge or skill, but flexible knowledge, flexible skills – those insights and abilities that enable us to learn new material quickly, to move easily from one job to another.

From 1940 to 1970 Americans experienced a period of rare economic supremacy. The G.I. Bill helped. So did the workplace entrance of American women, increasing by millions our own raw numbers of thinking workers. Manufacturing boomed on the strength of innovation, better markets and improved productivity. A baby-boom generation of workers came to expect ever-higher wages and non-competitive markets raising their standard of living so they could finance constantly larger homes in that new, American invention – the suburb.

What Americans mostly created others largely perfected. Japan and Germany have enjoyed tremendous economic revivals following World War Two and, in large measure, they did it with U.S. aid and

Illustration 4. Current Demographics for Leading Economic Producers per Area.

	China	India	U.S.
Internet Users in 2002 (millions)	94.0	18.5	159
Patents applied for in 2001	16,000	78,000	166,000
Gross Domestic Product/per capita (U.S. Dollars)	$5,600	$3,100	$40,100
National Gross Domestic Product	$7.262 trillion	$3.319 trillion	$11.750 trillion

Source: *CIA World Fact Book,* 2005.

knowledge. But for sheer speed of economic gain, note (in *Illustration 4*) what India and China have done with their GDPs based almost solely on improved knowledge among a large number of their people.

The engine driving the global economy, and pushing the speed with which competitor nations move past one another, is knowledge. If I graduated from high school in 1968 or even 1978 (when answering machines were novel and the fax was not yet known), I went to work to support my family, raise the children and plan for retirement. My learning was ended and my career lay before me. At least, so I assumed.

Early in the 1980s a report entitled *A Nation at Risk* eloquently called America to comprehensive education reform with "lifelong and continuous learning" fostered by partnerships between business, government and education. We now know the report was right. The "career employee" who retires from the company that first employed her is as rare as a nudist in a mosquito colony. Once told to expect seven careers in a professional lifetime, that number is now 10 to 14. We leave school ready, arguably, for the first one.

America is not just in a global economy, we're in the lead. But we're challenged to keep pace with the education offered in other nations. Our future competitiveness depends on our workforce, and the quality of our workforce depends on education.

At least five nations (New Zealand, United Kingdom, Norway, Finland, and the Netherlands) graduate a higher percent with bachelor's degrees than the U.S. In 2001 India graduated almost a million more college students than did the U.S., including 100,000 more in the sciences and 60,000 more in engineering. In 2004 China graduated almost twice as many students from college as did the U.S. (2.5 million vs. 1.3 million), in part because China understands better than the U.S. that higher education is the platform from which to build a sound economy via a skilled workforce.[29] We do not help ourselves by blaming them for being right.

Morgan Stanley's Stephen Roach recalled earlier American revolutions and summarized our challenge this way:

> *Our virtues lie in a flexible and open, technology friendly, risk-taking, entrepreneurial, market-driven system. This is exactly the same type of challenge farmers went through in the late 1800s, sweatshop workers went through in the early 1900s, and manufacturing workers experienced in the first half of the 1980s. We've got to focus on setting in motion a debate that pushes us into new sources of job creation rather than bemoaning the loss.*[30]

We cannot win in the world by hiding. We need to move out with confidence, even eagerness, for the competition that is ours to win.

Many forces brought Moscow to heel in the late 1980s but none more than world-wide technology. As Chernobyl melted down and its radioactive clouds drifted over Europe, party leaders in USSR central offices denied it all. As they lied, ordinary people across Soviet-dominated Eastern Europe turned on their televisions and watched the truth. Walls could make escape difficult, and had for a half-century. But no wall could keep out the truth, not any more, thanks to a French satellite beaming pictures from high above Chernobyl.

America, more than any nation in history or on earth, has the resources with which to educate and train the most competent workforce imaginable.

America, more than any nation in history or on earth, has the resources with which to educate and train the most competent workforce imaginable. What we have lacked is the candor to admit that this is a need and the will to invest what it will take to do the job.

If we collectively understand what this revolution has brought us, and if we collectively respond with the same spirit that has carried us through earlier revolutions, then by far the best days for America's workplaces and workers await us in the future.

Chapter Four

Shortage of Workers, Shortage of Skills

Today we have too many people willing to work in America. Tomorrow we will not have enough people to fill the available jobs, and people who *are* available will not have the right skills – unless we do something today.

The reality is that dramatic growth of the American workforce is over. Economic and population growth in the U.S. have climbed more or less in tandem. The combination of baby boomers, immigrants and working women has helped swell our workforce by 1.6 percent per year for the past 50 years. But during the coming 50 years America's workforce will grow by approximately 0.6 percent annually, about one-third the pace set over the last half-century. We know why.

> *The most inescapable challenge facing the American workforce in the coming twenty years is that, barring substantial change, we will not have enough people to fill it.*

First, we have been emptying a vast pool of American women who had previously been kept out of the workplace. The surplus in this pool has been drained.

Second, our workforce is aging. One out of eight Americans working today (13 percent) is over 55 years of age and this segment will balloon to 20 percent by 2020. Meanwhile, the share of the workforce aged 45 and older will increase from 33 percent in 1998 to 40 percent by 2008. Because this is so large a share of

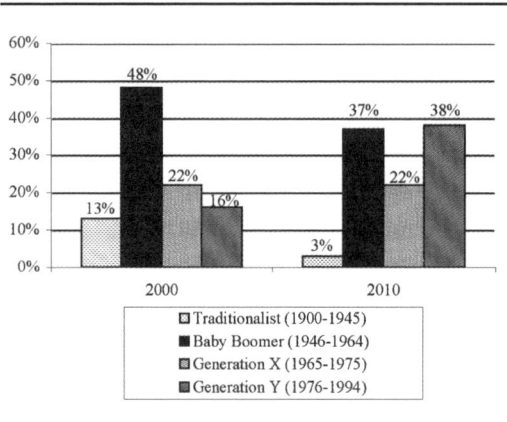

Illustration 5. Civilian Labor Force by Generation.

Source: Bureau of Labor Statistics.

the workforce, this 7 percent of increased growth will add nearly 17 million workers to this age group.[31]

Aging produces the numbers that fill *Illustration 5.* It charts the largest transition of workers from one generation to the next in American history. By 2030, while 46 million new workers enter the workforce, an unprecedented 76 million workers will enter retirement. Herein lies a crisis or two.

The fallout of this transition – 76 million workers out and 46 million in – is obvious. The available workforce will fall dramatically short of what's needed, beginning around the year 2010. And the number of retirees expecting others to pay for their extended lives through programs such as Social Security will boggle all government arithmetic.

Third, immigration can no longer make up the difference. Half the American labor-force growth during the 1990s came from immigration.[32]

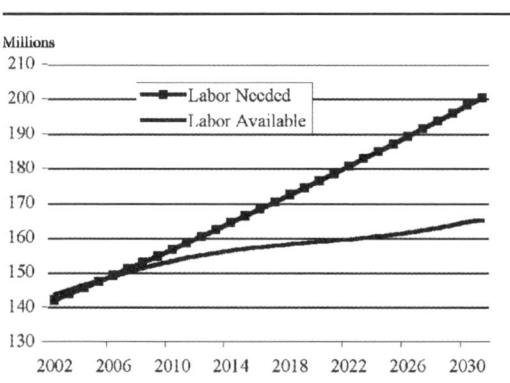

Illustration 6. Expected Labor Force and Labor Force Demand, 2002-2031.

Source: Employment Policy Foundation analysis and projections of Census/BLS and BEA data.

Between 1980 and 2000 our native-born workforce grew by 44 percent, but from 2000 to 2020 our native-born workforce will not grow at all. (Illegal immigration has produced in the range of 10 million new workers, but few *illegal* immigrants are equipped for higher-skill jobs in the new economy.)

The most inescapable challenge facing the American workforce in the coming twenty years is that, barring substantial change, we will not have enough people to fill it.

The second most telling challenge is that those available will not have the necessary skills. Anthony Carnevale offered the National Association of Manufacturing (NAM) a set of sobering comparisons between the so-called "Worker Gap" and "Skill Gap." As *Illustration 7* shows, the American workforce will have a *worker* gap of 7 million by 2010, climbing to over 20 million by 2020, and an alarming two-thirds of this shortage is a *skilled*-worker gap. If we used historic trend lines as our basis of projections, we face a 35-million worker shortfall by 2030.[33]

Illustration 7. Projected Skilled and Unskilled Worker Gap in 2010 and 2020.

	2010	2020
Skilled Worker Gap	5.3 million	14 million
Unskilled Worker Gap	1.7 million	7 million
Total Skilled & Unskilled Worker Gap	7 million	21 million

Source: Anthony Carnevale, NAM White Paper, Reported in Business 2.com.

Explanations of this data are not always what we would expect. "Despite the slow economic recovery in manufacturing," for example, "80 percent of manufacturers continue to experience a moderate to serious shortage of qualified job candidates."[34] Manufacturing, like every other field, needs workers capable of renewing their education to accommodate technological change and global competition. Brains beat brawn.

In practically every work site a post-secondary education already matters and will matter more as global competition demands more of us. So, for example, auto mechanics were once trained mostly through dirty, hands-on experience. But with modern innovations in technology, a mechanic's work is now 80 percent diagnostic and 20 percent repair. Automotive repair has become a field in which certification is required before the hood is lifted. A high school education and years in the grease pit are not enough any more.

Employment in the American (and global) workplace is increasingly reserved for the skilled. In the decade between 1992 and 2002 we witnessed a decrease in jobs for those with less than a high school degree, and a small increase for those with high school diplomas. Not everyone must have a four-year college degree. But almost everyone needs some post-secondary education and training to succeed in the future. Two-year, post-high school training produced almost seven million new jobs in the past decade. Four-year degrees produced just over six million new jobs. Together they account for over 80 percent of the job growth in the past decade. The assumption here is that education equals skills, and mostly it does.

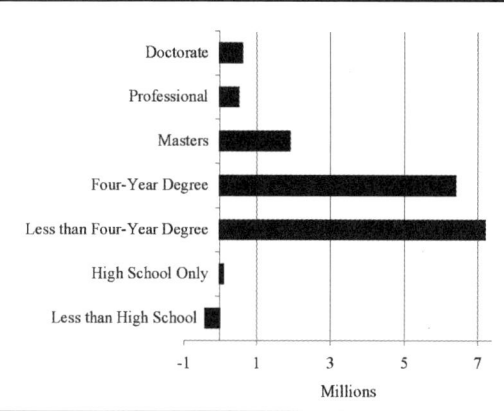

Illustration 8. Employment Change by Education, 1992-2002.

Source: Employment Policy Foundation tabulations of Bureau of Labor Statistics/Census Current Population Survey data; MTC Institute.

Using accepted workforce terminology, "professionals" are those with four-year college degrees, "skilled workers" include all with two-years of training or experience, and "unskilled" is reserved for those with a high school education or less.

By these definitions, nearly 60 percent of all American jobs were available to the unskilled in 1950. But by 1991 that 60 percent had fallen to 45 percent and during the 1990s it went over the cliff, falling to some 15 percent of all openings. By 2015, 76 percent of American workers are expected to have completed education equipping themselves for skilled or professional posts.[35]

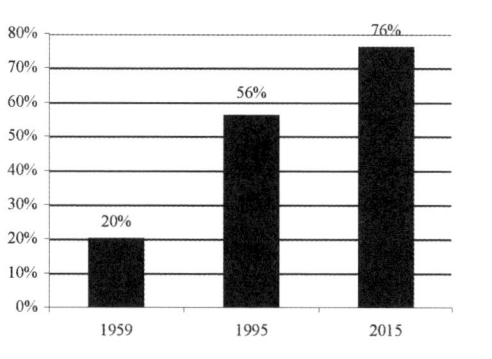

Illustration 9. Percent of Workers with Some Postsecondary Training, 1959 to 2015.

Source: Carnevale, Anthony P. and Richard A. Fry. *Crossing the Great Divide.* Educational Testing Services, 2000.

It's already the case in America that more education equates to less unemployment. High school drop-outs have an unemployment rate (9.40 percent) nearly twice the level of high school graduates (5.45 percent), more than three times the unemployment rate of college graduates (3.10 percent).[36]

And earnings returned on work highlight the escalating difference education makes in employment. In 1980 college graduates earned 50 percent more during their lifetime than high school grads. Today, this earning differential has increased to 100 percent and continues to expand. Increased income directly corresponds to increased education beginning with high school and moving upward with a vocational certificate, some college and an associate's degree. In 2003 an individual with less than a high school diploma earned an average annual salary of $22,200, compared to someone with an associate's degree who was earning on average $37,482.[37]

America faces a future in which we have too few workers and, especially, too few skilled workers. This is a certainty, not a guess, unless we make substantial and immediate changes. We can alter the outcome of the jobs revolution, including this crisis, if we act now.

What we hear is not a giant sucking sound from south of the border; it's the squeaking of the window of opportunity as it slowly, certainly, closes in front of us. We need leaders to champion a sense of urgency, and champion it soon, if we want America to compete in the global marketplace, and win.

Chapter Five

New Faces in the Workplace

The United States, unlike any other nation in the world, increasingly reflects the world's diverse populations. The American ideal is more and more an opportunity, not just a dream, for men and women of all races and colors and religions.

The story of diversity in the American workplace is already being told. While the labor force before 1998 was 40 percent white male and 25 percent minority, these ratios have shifted. The rate of workforce growth for Hispanics, for example, is more than eight times greater than for Whites during the current decade.

Illustration 10. Annual Workforce Growth Rates in the United States between 2002 and 2012.

Ethnicity	Percent Growth per Year
White, non-Hispanic	0.3%
Black	1.8%
Asian	4.2%
Hispanic	2.9%

Source: Bureau of Labor Statistics Labor Review February 2004, Labor Force Projections to 2012.

If we take an even longer national view, the numbers foretell powerful and promising workforce diversity – see *Illustration 11* – yet even this table, drawing on 2000 Census projections, is outdated. In the first two years after the census the Hispanic population in America grew almost 9 percent. Such growth suggests America will become a minority-majority nation much sooner than 2050. Regionally, in places like California, differences will emerge even more quickly.

Blacks will play a prominent role in the U.S. South's economy and Hispanics will impact the West. The Northeast continues as the most diverse region, including significant numbers of all racial and ethnic workers, while the Midwest remains the least diverse. The next few years of the jobs revolution is, for minorities, a "good news, bad news" scenario. Our nation's minorities are positioned to benefit from growing career opportunities and earnings potential.

Minority populations are growing fastest and so are jobs built on technology, and technology is a great leveler of people because computers do not care whose fingers work the keyboards. Technology's indifference to the nation in which it is used has helped foster global competition. That same indifference to the color and religion of users enables personal freedom to grow by leaps and bounds, also within the U.S. All that someone needs is education and training.

Ah, but there's the rub: "education and training." Victory in the jobs revolution will fall to those with the most knowledge and skills (read: education), and minorities are losing the educational race in America today.

Initial test data collected by schools complying with the recent federal legislation, *No Child Left Behind*,

Illustration 11. Percent of Workforce by Ethnic Group 2003 to 2050.

Ethnicity	2003	2010	2050
White	73%	65%	53%
Hispanic	11%	16%	24%
Black	12%	13%	14%
Asian	5%	7%	11%

Source: Bureau of Labor Statistics Monthly Labor Review May 2002, A century of change: The U.S. labor force, 1950-2050.

shows that educational achievement in America is not equal. Minority students lag badly. In 2000, 34 percent of Asian students, 20 percent of White students, 9 percent of American Indian students, 4 percent of Hispanic students and 3 percent of Black students were proficient at the 12th grade level of math.[38] As a result of these discrepancies, many students give up and drop out, leaving a sorry statistic to haunt us all: Ninety-seven percent of Hispanic workers enter the American workforce without a college degree. Overlay this reality with another: Between the time of this writing and the year 2025, 93 percent of the *growth* in school-aged children in America will be Hispanic.

A 2004 study by The Urban Institute projected that of all the students who entered ninth grade in 1999, only 68 percent were expected to graduate within four years. The study goes on to suggest that only 50 percent of Blacks, 51 percent of Native Americans and 53 percent of Hispanics will receive their high school diplomas.[39]

Illustration 12. Workforce by Region and Ethnicity, 2015.

Region	White	Black	Hispanic
Northeast	70%	11%	13%
Midwest	81%	11%	5%
South	65%	20%	13%
West	53%	3%	29%

Source: U.S Census Bureau, Mathamatica 2001 National Job Corps Study, Bureau of Justice Statistics, MTCI.

Our ability to succeed as a nation is quickly becoming dependent upon our ability to educate, train, place, retain and compensate a diverse workforce. We appear, at the moment, to be faltering.[40]

College enrollment data supplies both hope and worry. Overall, the percent of high school graduates who enroll in college has increased significantly since 1972. When viewed across racial and ethnic populations, 64 percent of White high school graduates enroll in college. College enrollment for Black students has increased 22 percent. Unfortunately, Hispanic enrollment increased by only 15 percent.[41]

During the 1990s total minority enrollment in college grew by 48 percent.[42] By the end of the 1990s over 10 million White students were enrolled in American colleges compared to 4 million minority students. This is an improvement over what we had before, but is still a disparity worth correcting since it doesn't reflect the racial or ethnic balance of the nation's youth.

More troubling, and largely unimproved, is ethnic data on college retention and graduation rates. We're relatively good, as a nation, at getting students into higher education. We are not nearly as successful at getting them to graduation. Some 85 percent of high school students graduate and, of these, roughly 60 percent go on to college. After six years, about 60 percent of those who enrolled in college emerge with a college degree. Do the math. If you start out with 100 high school students, about 33 of them will obtain a college degree and most will be Anglo.[43] That's what is troubling.

As minorities become increasingly dominant in the workforce, failures in minority education will flood into the workplace. Hispanics are disproportionately dropping out of high school. At the "high" end, only 11 percent of Hispanics over the age of 25 have a bachelor's degree (compared to 47 percent of Asians, 17 percent of Blacks and 27 percent of Whites).[44] And Hispanics are the fastest-growing group coming into the workforce.

In 2001 America counted 27.2 million young adults (aged 18-24). If we look at population forecasts, young-adult demographics tell us that by 2010 Hispanics will comprise 37 percent of the new workforce age group, Whites will comprise 31 percent and Blacks will make up 19 percent.[45] Therefore, we will experience greatest growth among those with greatest educational failure rates today, and this will continue as the workforce ages.

America's present workforce lacks the symbols of justice and equal opportunity, and the numbers tell us we're charting a course to a crisis. We need today's minority children to become tomorrow's skilled and professional workers. It's an economic as well as social imperative. We cannot afford to waste these lives if we want America to compete effectively in the global marketplace. Based on today's educational data, it appears we're stumbling at the starting gate in the race for competitiveness.

Victory in the jobs revolution will fall to those with the most knowledge and skills (read: education), and minorities are losing the educational race in America today.

We may be doing better with older adults. During the two decades from 1971 to 1991, college enrollment of students 25 years and older increased by over 171 percent. The majority of this increase came from 30-34 year olds, although 25-29 year olds contributed a 99 percent gain and those above age 35 increased by another 48 percent.[46] By comparison, during this time the U.S. population increased by only 21 percent.[47]

Explanations for why more adults are enrolling in college vary. Many American adults have more leisure time and more disposable income; these factors may matter. One study suggests that employers may have encouraged such attendance to help maintain a capable workforce.[48] Drucker concluded that, with the U.S. in the information-age, employees can see that knowledge workers dominate their organizations.[49] States have increasingly imposed requirements for a broad array of professionals to continue their education; this could have boosted adult college enrollments.[50] And some studies show a generally heightened enthusiasm for adults to engage in learning activities; maybe adults went to college in increasing numbers because they wanted to. Whatever the reason, older adults enrolling in college may bode well for older employees in the workforce.

Education is the key but work habits are still critical. A diploma of some kind opens doors. But once inside, America's future workforce, especially minority youth, is terribly challenged. While national unemployment has hovered between 5 and 6 percent in recent years, youth unemployment is almost three times higher: It stood at 17.7 percent, for example, in April 2005. Some experts attribute increased youth unemployment to the loss of low-paying and entry-level jobs to immigrants, especially illegal immigrants. Perhaps.

Illustration 13. Percent of Youth Age 16-19 Unemployed.

Ethnicity	Percent Youth Unemployment
White (incl. Hispanic)	15.3%
Black	35.5%
Hispanic*	18.6%
Total Youth	17.7%

Source: Bureau of Labor Statistics, April 2005.
* Not Seasonally Adjusted

Whatever the cause, the consequences of vast youth unemployment are devastating. It means we have a generation of needed employees who are not learning the fundamental work habits that keep them employed: getting out of bed, coming to work drug-free, on-time and dressed appropriately, speaking language that fits the employer's culture.

Combining educational failure rates with youth unemployment rates, we cannot escape an ugly conclusion: We're creating multiple barriers to successful employment for the next generation of workers. We are treating them, as a group, to a famine in education, skills, and work habits needed for their success and for ours.

Raul Yzaguirre, President of La Raza, America's largest Hispanic organization, recently reminded us that "the education gap between the Hispanic and the majority community is not narrowing, it's getting wider." If we want to win any economic competition in the global arena, America can simply not afford to have this continue. Here is a national interest in which we should be more than interested.

American women in the workplace have charted a vastly more positive course. As women's educational levels have climbed, and barriers of discrimination have lowered, women are increasingly taking up management and professional occupations from 30 percent of the workforce in 1970 to 50 percent in 2000.

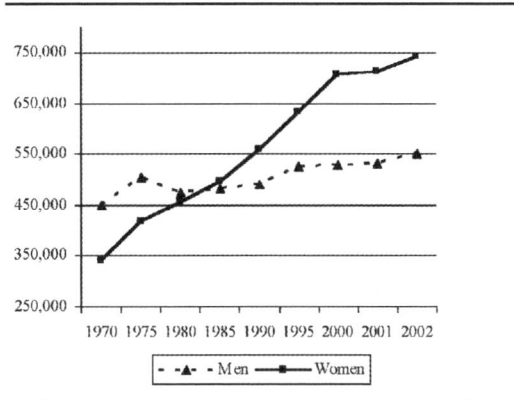

Illustration 14. Bachelor's Degrees Awarded to Men and Women, 1970 to 2002.

Source: National Center for Education Statistics, Digest of Education Statistics, 2003.

High school drop-out rates for women have declined 38 percent since 1972 (from 15 percent to 9 percent). In 2001, fewer women than men dropped out of high school (9 percent compared to more than 12 percent)[51] with drop-out rates decreasing over these three decades for both Black and White women.

The most shocking gender statistic is found on college campuses. A four-year college degree is a vast predictor of career success and high-income returns. American women apparently understand this better than men. College men outnumbered women ten to seven (5 million to 3.5 million) in 1970. By 1979 the two genders were matched at 5.6 million each. By 2002 women had passed men in college enrollments by a net 2.1 million (9.1 million to 7.0 million).[52] Women have not only enrolled; they've graduated. In every single year since 1985 women have been awarded more bachelor's degrees than men; every year. By 2002 the disparity was enormous: 742,000 women received degrees compared to 549,800 men.[53]

The shadow side of this story is a quiet but growing decline in male workers. In spite of looming shortages, men are opting out of the labor force. The Center for Labor Market Studies at Northeastern University in Boston produced a comprehensive study on "The Absent Male Worker and the Limited Growth in New England's Labor Force in the 1990s." The report points out that, in 1970, 73 percent of all men ages 45-69 were employed full-time in Massachusetts. By 1996-97, only 56 percent were employed on a full-time basis.[54] While this study focuses on one geographic area, its underlying message is broader than just one state.

America's pattern of imprisonment impacts men disproportionately, especially young men, and more especially young minority men. In 1972 U.S. federal and state prisons held about 200,000 inmates; by 2000 they housed more than 1.3 million. Nearly one-third of prison inmates today are non-violent drug offenders

We're creating multiple barriers to successful employment for the next generation of workers. We are treating them, as a group, to a famine in education, skills, and work habits needed for their success and ours.

serving "mandatory minimum" sentences that effectively remove them forever from the American workforce.

Global competitiveness is already driven by brain power and entrepreneurial drive. Corporate America cannot afford to, and will not, discriminate on the basis of racial, ethnic, gender or other grounds. In the place of historic bias and old barriers will be open doors of opportunity with entrance limited only by an individual's education, skill and initiative. But education, skill and initiative are not being spread equally across all racial and ethnic youth today.

For the private sector to fill the nation's employment ranks, we must win the jobs revolution long before employment beckons, before kindergarten. Today, especially in growing communities of minorities and immigrants, this is where we are most at risk of losing hope, talent, and the nation's ability to compete long term.

Chapter Six

Looking for a Job?

For all the headlines about exported jobs and unfair global competition, America's economy is doing well. Those of us with a strong education and flexible job skills are, mostly, doing well too. But even we must recognize that not all is tranquil in the jobs market. In fact, U.S. jobs are churning at an unprecedented rate mostly because of America's position in the broader, global market. As the wizened and wise Alan Greenspan has told us,

> *The sensitivity of our economy to foreign competition does appear to have intensified recently.... A million workers leave their jobs every week, two-fifths involuntarily, often in association with facilities that have been displaced or abandoned. A million, more or less, are also newly hired or returned from lay-offs every week, in part as new facilities come on stream.*[55]

Between 1992 and 1999 America increased its exports 56 percent to a total of $960.3 billion. During this same period American jobs related to exports increased by 17 percent, to 11.5 million. Greenspan's point is correct: Global competition (trade) takes away some jobs, which we regret, but it adds even more jobs, a reality too easily ignored or dismissed in the jobs debate.

If we want jobs, we must get American businesses up close to global competitors. Automobile dealerships build next door to each other. Why? Because they reach a larger share of the market by being within eyesight of their competition. They want a share of their competitor's market and the only way to get it is by being present in that market. So they move in.

The same thing is true in a global marketplace. What we want to do as American business is get closer to, not farther from, our foreign competitors. They own a market where we want a presence. The stronger we are there, the more jobs we have here.

We need to see ourselves in the global economy not as victims but as competitors. If China, for example, is raising the standard of living for a hundred million people – and it is – then our market can be expanded by 100 million. All we need to do is get in.

Just as electricity reduced the role of American candle makers, and the automobile reduced the role of carriage makers, today's economy will reduce the role of outmoded occupations in America.

The new American workplace is already and increasingly a workstation located in the U.S. but with a market that knows no boundaries. By being in the global market, we do face more competitors but we also access more buyers. With buyers, come jobs.

But these won't be our fathers' jobs. Just as electricity reduced the role of American candle makers, and the automobile reduced the role of carriage makers, today's economy is reducing the role of outmoded occupations in America. At the same time, new jobs are being created in response to this new economy, and access to these jobs is and will be available through education and training.

Job churning happens at rates far, far above what most of us imagine. The venerable *Washington Post* (March 4, 2004) reminded us all that capitalism "eliminates jobs constantly, but except during recessions it creates new ones even more quickly: In 1999 alone, 33 million jobs were destroyed and 36 million were created."

In earlier times, particularly during the 1980s and '90s, our attention and frustration with global competition focused exclusively on the transfer of manufacturing jobs to other parts of the world. We explained the loss of manufacturing jobs as the transfer of unskilled work to *lower*-skilled and lower-paying economies. Now we are witnessing a new paradigm, the transfer of skilled, white-collar jobs to other parts of the globe – jobs moving into *higher*-skilled, lower-paying economies.

Illinois Congressman Don Manzullo asked at a recent hearing, "Can America lose these white-collar jobs and still prosper?" A new study by McKinsey suggests optimistically that the answer is "Yes." Eventually, the U.S. economy will receive at least two-thirds of the benefit from outsourcing offshore to lower-wage nations (from reduced prices for goods and services consumed in the U.S., higher profits reinvested back home, and new markets in foreign countries for other U.S. goods and services).[56] But the "eventually" in the preceding sentence recognizes that some U.S. workers will be unemployed by the transition. For them, the answer lacks optimism.

If today's student wants to be the hot commodity in tomorrow's workplace, she should stay in school. We'll have 30 million skilled-worker slots and 23 million Americans to fill them.

Ray Uhalde of the National Center on Education and the Economy (NCEE) has labored with distinction in workforce training programs through decades of recession, plant closings, trade agreements, job dislocations and other economic challenges. Speaking to the National Governors Association Workforce Development Conference, he recently put the transition of jobs in a positive perspective.

> *It isn't true that there are only so many good jobs to go around in this world. Knowledge development through the process of R&D, discovery, innovation, and problem solving, and the arts of product development and mass marketing present endless possibilities for satisfying the limitless needs of people throughout the world. More good jobs will follow more good ideas for satisfying and improving the human condition.*[57]

What we need to do, if we want more jobs in America, is shorten the transition time between when jobs leave the U.S. and when new jobs are created to take their place. Uhalde's formula for achieving this trick is right on. It takes American discovery, innovation, problem solving and so forth.

What it will *not* take is higher trade barriers. No country has ever permanently increased jobs, standards of living or broad social justice for its people through either external or internal economic constraints. These strategies could not save even the jobs of candle makers or carriage builders. Retreats from the world market lead to defeat, not victory.

We talk about "the economy" but what we mean is "my paycheck." We worry about "education" but what we mean is "my child's ability to hold a job."

As in earlier revolutions, this one demands that we go forward, not long for return to a happier utopian moment. What's different in this revolution is that the world market is brought to us 24-hours-a-day courtesy of CNN and MSNBC and a growing family of international broadcasters. Change in this revolution is coming at break-neck speed. Technology barely introduces one advance before the next comes streaking over the horizon. We are exhausted by it. It's natural that we want to stop, get off the globe and see if our fathers' jobs aren't still lurking somewhere in the neighborhood.

Inevitably and already the global economy is redefining America's workplace. But it is a redefinition, not an elimination.

Job growth is down in American manufacturing, mostly as a result of productivity gains. But job growth is decidedly up in construction, transportation, trade, financial and insurance services, business services, medical services, education, professional services and public administration. Each of these sectors has experienced growth of between 50,000 and 300,000 jobs in the past decade, and each projects an increase of between 750,000 and 4 million new jobs in the decade ahead.

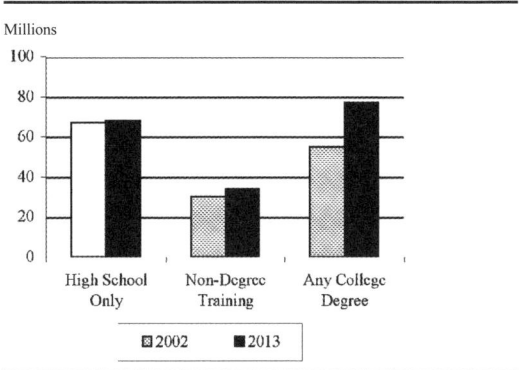

Illustration 15. New Jobs Will Require More Education, New Employment by Education 2002 and Projected 2013.

The only group of Americans consistently losing jobs over the past decade was the population that did not finish high school. Job growth was modest for those who graduated high school and significant for those with college and, especially, degrees.

If trends matter, and they do, then those who want jobs need to reckon with a single, thundering reality: Job growth over the next decade will occur in professions requiring at least some level of college certificate and/or degree. Expanding job markets and higher wage scales will continue to travel together. In short, for individual workers, increased education and training will produce more job choices and higher compensation.

Millions of jobs will remain available for those with high school diplomas or less. But, these jobs will continue to decline in both real numbers and as a percent of total jobs. As they decline in demand, they are likely also to decline in wages and benefits.

But if today's student wants to be the hot commodity in tomorrow's workplace, she should stay in school. By 2012, we're going to come up short 848,000 more workers with two-year degrees than we produce, 3.3 million more workers with four-year degrees than we educate, and 2.9 million more workers with advanced degrees than we graduate. In sum, we'll come up short more than 7 million skilled workers.

Every unfilled job translates to products and services we cannot deliver to the global market and, therefore, dollars we cannot return to the U.S. economy. Almost certainly, jobs unfilled in the U.S. will go elsewhere and not return.

A shortage of workers gives some comfort to the unemployed and, perhaps, some advantage to those seeking jobs. But in terms of national interest, a worker shortage of these proportions is a calamity. Every unfilled job translates to products and services we cannot deliver to the global market and, therefore, dollars we cannot return to the U.S. economy. Almost certainly, jobs unfilled in the U.S. will go elsewhere and not return.

"Looking for a job? Get an education." It's so simple we can't help but wonder why it's not being touted as the obvious first step toward America's triumph in the jobs revolution.

We are a nation more than ever dependent on leaders who will tell the truth, set an honest course toward competing in a global economy, and advocate policies that protect those at-risk: minorities whose education is faltering, aging workers fearful that old dogs can't learn new tricks, the unemployed who've given up on themselves and our economy.

Trade and economic policies are traditional political battlefields. But one area where consensus *should* occur is in the public response to workers who will be or already are displaced by global trade. The public sector, in partnership with business and education, *should* assist individual workers to prepare for their jobs, upgrade their skills while on the job and develop new skills for future jobs.

Americans being polled for 2004 election preferences identified the economy, education, health care and global trade as key issues. What they're actually ranking are symptoms of the changing American workforce. We talk about "the economy" but what we mean is "my paycheck." We worry about "education" but what we mean is "my child's ability to hold a job." Even worries about "health care" are, for most Americans, worries about employer-sponsored health insurance.

Solutions are within reach. If we had adequate preparation, that is, education for all our workers, most of the hovering economic and social crises would be vastly diminished.

We hear a great deal about national security and national interest these days. Our security as a nation will be challenged in ways we've not yet imagined if we fail to solve the crises affecting our workforce. Our national interest will be met when our educational goals are aligned to the changing workplace, and are met.

Chapter Seven

Taking Jobs to Market

Micheline Maynard has covered the automobile industry for United Press International (UPI) for two decades and recently authored *The End of Detroit: How the Big Three Lost Their Grip on the American Car Market*. In a post-publication interview Maynard summarized the change in the automotive workplace.

> *Actually, the US auto industry isn't in decline. We now have two American auto industries: the traditional industry, led by Detroit's Big Three, and the new industry, dominated by foreign companies. It's sad to see the traditional industry lose ground, but the emergence of the new industry has only been to the benefit of customers. And I believe the traditional industry is getting more efficient, thanks to the presence of foreign competition.*[58]

If the changes in an industry are good for the market, are they also good for the workers? It's a vexing question in part because of timing: What the market demands often causes a decline or slump in workforce gains, even though market responsiveness eventually generates more jobs and more revenues.

When electricity first arrived, candle makers went unemployed; soon, jobs in the electrical industry vastly outnumbered unemployed candle makers. For candle makers, the change was painful. For the workforce as a whole, the change was growth.

51

General Motors annually produces about the same number of cars today that it did at the height of the domestic auto industry, five million. But in 2004 it produced those cars with 118,000 employees, a reduction of 336,000 workers from its peak employment.

The decline in the number of workers was driven by better process engineering and improved technology, including robotics. Between better machinery, better processes and better skills, the outcome was better productivity.

Many of the 336,000 workers no longer building cars have retired (the automotive workforce was, for various reasons, among the oldest in America). Of those still working, the majority went to positions supporting the automotive industry: innovative suppliers of automotive parts. But there were also casualties especially among those with the least education and the lowest skill sets.

General Motors annually produces about the same number of cars today that it did at the height of the domestic auto industry, five million. But today it produces those cars with 118,000 employees, a reduction of 336,000 workers from its peak employment.

The worldwide market for American cars has grown as the economies of other nations have risen. China's economy goes up, and so does the number of people eager to trade in bikes for autos. (While American car sales grew at a 2 percent clip in 2003, China's sales recorded double-digit growth.)[59] What was once an American market is now a global market. In order for American auto companies to succeed, productivity gains must continue and access to China's market must be (and is being) gained. It is all part of the changing markets that are changing jobs.

In 2003 the American GDP increased 3.1 percent with almost a half-million less Americans working than in 2002. Manufacturing led the nation in job declines

(516,000) while health care, finance, engineering and management, along with state and local governments, posted significant job increases. Increases in jobs generally trail increases in market demand.

The "economy of jobs" will soon be clear in places like China. Life on the farm is grueling and antiquated in China. No wonder industry and services have beckoned nearly 100 million laborers who've moved into cities for factory or office work. China's factory workers earn three times the salary of most Chinese farmers. Because life on the farm is so desperate, low-wage jobs in factories are comparatively attractive. Thus, while Chinese manufacturers typically lack American productivity, they are able to compete with the U.S. through low wages. But as soon as technology finds its way to all areas of the Chinese workplace, at least to the extent that workers are free to choose, the Chinese workplace will begin to show patterns already seen in the U.S.[60] Factory jobs will go empty until wages go up because the market for jobs works just like the market for products: If no one wants it (a product or a job), you cannot give it away.

Global markets are clearly changing the available jobs in all parts of the world. Just as Europe lost manufacturing jobs to America after World War Two, the U.S. is now yielding similar jobs to lower-cost labor in other parts of the world. Americans shop at discount stores for the lowest-priced products, sending the signal that we *do* want low-cost production. The global market hears the siren call, and responds.

The Federal Reserve of Dallas did a comparison of global, hourly manufacturing payrolls in 2001 and discovered wages stacked on four tiers. Tier One includes Japan, the U.S. and Europe. Tier Two has Singapore, Korea and Taiwan. Mexico and Brazil fill Tier Three and China is alone at Tier Four.

These findings position American jobs in the worldwide workforce market. We can't compete with 64 cents an hour unless our productivity is 3,000 percent higher – which, in some instances, it is. (American agriculture competes effectively with China's because one U.S. farm worker produces more output than 31 Chinese farm workers.) Even so, as Edward Greenberg and Leon Grunberg have observed, "Fundamental transformations now underway in the global economy have compelled large corporations to develop new strategies with respect to both their external environment and their internal operations to enhance competitiveness."[61] That's a very complicated way of saying, "In this market the kinds of jobs we create will change."

Greenberg and Grunberg have shown that American job cuts rarely result from global competition. The two strategies most employed by American companies are reductions in raw goods costs and constant innovation in the design, production and marketing of products. "For employees, this generally means 'reengineering' existing jobs – learning new skills, or using skills in unfamiliar settings or tasks, changing standard operating procedures, increased responsibility

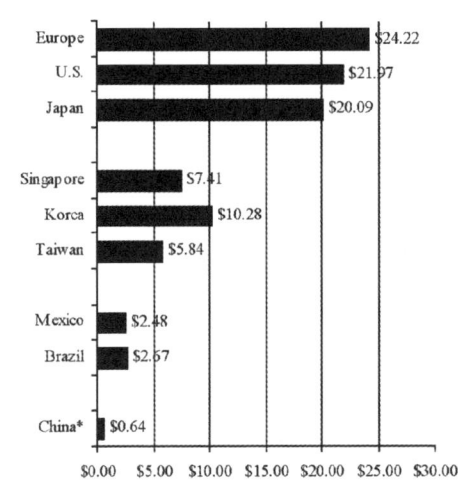

Illustration 16. Global Manufacturing Hourly Wages, 2003.

Europe	$24.22
U.S.	$21.97
Japan	$20.09
Singapore	$7.41
Korea	$10.28
Taiwan	$5.84
Mexico	$2.48
Brazil	$2.67
China*	$0.64

Source: Bureau of Labor Statistics, Foreign Labor Statistics Report, November 2004. *Just How Cheap is Chinese Labor?, *BusinessWeek,* December 2, 2004.

for autonomous action, result-based compensation, and an intensification of work (longer hours, more pressures to produce results) – and, very often, becoming members of 'work teams.'"[62] For very, very few workers does foreign competition spell inevitable unemployment.

Even if markets are firm and trends are reliable, anxiety is high. The U.S. Bureau of Labor Statistics (BLS) has for decades provided accurate, unbiased analysis and information on the American economy. Since October of 2001 the BLS has offered monthly surveys of job openings and turnovers for each major industry sector. It shifted to this strategy because it saw the American workforce struggling with rapid change.

> *There is continued concern that employment relationships are becoming less secure. The temporary help industry has grown more rapidly than many other sectors of the economy. Further, in 1997, six million workers viewed their main job as contingent, believing that they lacked a commitment for ongoing employment in that job. In addition, millions of workers are displaced from their jobs each year because of structural changes in the economy.*[63]

The most secure institutions of our childhood – government, schools, banks, churches – seem, sometimes, to have lost their bearings. We wonder what and who we can trust. We worry about work and insurance and retirement. Our jobs are a source of anxiety as much as income.

Our grandparents didn't play computer games. They had a fraction of the healthcare options and services we enjoy today. And their education was likely to have stopped years short of what we and our children expect. But our grandparents seemed more satisfied, even if we are better off.

Some studies suggest that jobs and wealth are increasingly dividing America into one class of people going lower and lower while another goes higher and higher. This may be so, although a more accurate way to describe it is that those with good knowledge and skills continue to improve while those lacking both fall farther and farther behind. To the extent this is true, shame on us for letting it happen; the American challenge is to equip all our citizens with the education and skills necessary to move forward.[64]

What we know is that, in America, it will be a workers' market. The more skilled the worker, the keener the competition for his or her services. Bidding wars for best employees may raise wages but reduce loyalty on both sides, the worker's and the employer's. In a thoughtful analysis, the Mackinac Center for Public Policy reported that "younger workers have little knowledge of, and do not particularly care about, unions. More than 70 percent of the current civilian labor force is under the age of 45. Today's workers also tend to be highly mobile, better educated and often in white-collar or new-collar careers. They care about wages, but many care more about such issues as career advancement, day care, quality of life on the job, developing new skills, and having some say in how their jobs are done."[65] They care very much about their paychecks, but they do not care greatly about the name of the company on their checks.

We must enable students to learn how to learn, over and over again.

The assumption of a "social contract" between employers and employees is gone. Our fathers had reason to believe that if they served their companies well, their companies would employ them into retirement. Our sons and daughters have no reason to hold such a belief, and neither do we. More than ever, our jobs appear based on a market we cannot control and our employment is rooted in whatever skills we've packed in our bag along the way.

The encouraging thing is that we, the workers, are increasingly in charge of our own futures. The fearful thing is the same: we are in charge, ready or not.

Chapter Eight

Education for Employment

The U.S. Department of Labor predicts that today's graduating students will have between 10 and 14 various careers in their lifetimes.[66] Such a dizzying array of careers may forestall boredom. But it makes preparation a daunting task. What should I tell my child to learn if there's no telling what she'll be doing five years into her career?

Former Secretary of Education Richard Riley recently noted that none of the top 10 jobs that will exist in 2010 exist today, and that these jobs will employ technology that hasn't yet been invented to solve problems we haven't yet imagined. So how do we equip learners to prepare? How can we train them in what hasn't yet been imagined?

The most important thing a student can master today is "learning to learn." If, facing a new challenge – an unimagined problem, a job they've never seen, a technology that's brand new – if in these settings they know how to organize their thinking, structure their questions, and go about the task of *learning*, they will succeed. By learning to learn, today's students can gain new skills, new knowledge, even new attitudes and behaviors needed to succeed at work and in life. Rather than focusing on specific technologies or specific problems, we need to equip students with those concepts that are common to all problems, all technologies, all skills[67] ranging from workplace engineering to ethics to entrepreneurship.

The U.S. Department of Labor suggests students learn the factors that reduce stress in the workplace. Why? Because, personally, more of us will face such stress and, professionally, emerging careers are likely to be based on "human factors engineering" – the design of workplaces that are as stress-free as possible. The goal is not only comfort but productivity (lessened tensions means fewer sick days, reduced conflict, stronger teams and lower costs per unit of work achieved).[68] Workplace engineering was not a major in any college attended by the authors of this book.

Liberal arts curricula have long contained philosophy courses including ethics. But not until the recent spate of corporate scandals did the "ethics officer" emerge as a career option. It's one now.

Learning for employment needs to be aligned with the future, not the past, and must accommodate change occurring in our world, and in our workplaces, at blinding speed.

In December of 1990 there was one web site. In December of 1996 there were 603,367. By 2000 there were 25,675,581. In December of 2004 there were 56,923,737.[69]

Skyrocketing growth of web sites is more than a statistical curiosity. It's a live demonstration of a change that is revolutionizing both the workplace and the education that equips us for work. New, web-based jobs have popped up at an astronomic rate. Hundreds of careers and millions of jobs have been created around "the web industry." A scant decade ago, we walked into libraries to do research. Today the key resource is a PC linked to – by the time this book gets printed – more than 57 million web sites.

From the perspective of formal, traditional educational institutions, the dynamic that is hardest to manage is *speed*. College and university curricula have been significantly revised at an historic rate of once per decade, largely paralleling the cycle of accreditation. Making modest adjustments once every ten years will not work in a jobs revolution that revamps fundamentals daily. Web-site growth illustrates the problem but doesn't solve it. It simply demonstrates that changing curricula and naming new courses once a decade won't do.

Knowledge is being outdated at rates that are still escalating. Even where knowledge is current when students graduate, it is soon outdated. While the number of new careers is increasing, the life-span of applicable knowledge is decreasing. College degrees maintain their relevancy for much shorter time periods. A bachelor's degree in business may now have a shelf-life of only five years. No wonder that lifelong learning has become the typical anthem for teachers and managers in both college and university business schools/departments and corporate universities.[70]

From the perspective of formal, traditional educational institutions, the dynamic that is hardest to manage is speed.

The Apollo Group, Inc., parent company of the University of Phoenix, which now enrolls more than 200,000 students, said in its 2001 Annual Report that "rapid changes in technology and economic organization have made life-long learning an imperative, an imperative that gives both employees and their employers a competitive advantage. It is also an imperative that rewards institutions providing education that is current, relevant, efficient, and accessible."[71] The University of Phoenix should know. It has been in recent years the fastest-growing, for-profit university in the world.

After years of cutting back on corporate training, U.S. businesses have reversed the trend. According to the American Society for Training & Development's (ASTD) 2003 State of the Industry Report, organizations in the U.S. invested more money on employee training, made more hours of training available to employees and utilized technology to deliver more training in 2002 than in any previous year.[72] According to ASTD's Director of Research, Brenda Sugrue, "these organizations understand that the key to sustaining a competitive advantage is a knowledgeable, highly skilled workforce."[73]

Increased corporate investment in learning is a positive sign. But it contains a not-very-subtle warning to traditional sources of higher education. American business investment in such training had been in decline (it fell 18 percent between 1988 and 1997). The rapid return to investment in this area may mean that colleges and universities wanting to partner with business have new opportunities – the trend in corporate training is toward outsourcing this function – and that institutions wanting to stay in the Ivory Tower may starve there.

The challenge to higher education is relevance. Someone once remarked that the only thing harder to move than a cemetery is a college faculty. This cruel cut is getting some credence as universities try to respond to the changing expectations of the economy, workplace and workforce. The National Center for Education Statistics reports that more than 500 institutions of higher education closed their doors in the past 10 years. At the same time corporate universities have grown exponentially to more than 2,000 in comparison with the 3,600 accredited universities in the United States.[74] "The

While the number of new careers is increasing, the life-span of applicable knowledge is decreasing. College degrees maintain their relevancy for much shorter time periods.

growing disparity between the struggles of the academic university versus the explosive growth of corporate universities points to the opportunity facing accredited universities – partner, or risk obsolescence."[75]

Some academicians have taken the position that they know best and, on their campus, "This is what we offer, take it or leave it." Elitism is not dead. But it's suffocating under a wave of institutions actively pursuing a strong customer-orientation, customizing the education they offer to fit the markets they serve.[76] Consider two examples:

> *John Deere partners with Indiana University Kelly School of Management to create customized electives for an MBA program with a specialty in finance. The program was designed to develop a critical mass of finance leaders at John Deere with a combination of financial technical skills and business acumen. The customized MBA created to fill this need was a blended offering mixing on-site and online delivery.*[77]

> *The University of Wisconsin-Stout is the first college in America to receive the Malcolm Baldrige Award for Excellence. When it first applied, the review panel informed the campus of a need to better engage its superb academic programs with the community's needs. Chancellor Charles Sorensen organized a visioning session between the university's leaders and the state's business and educational leadership to find UW-Stout's best strategy for meeting the public need in the decade ahead. When the course was clear, Sorensen and his colleagues risked considerable change to earn the Award it received.*

Community and technical colleges are uniquely positioned to respond to immediate employment needs in their respective communities. Today, over 1,150 public, private and tribal community colleges serve over 11.6 million students.[78] More than half of the growth in postsecondary enrollment since 1970 has occurred at two-year institutions.[79] Credit and non-credit programs each attract about 50 percent of the student body. Because the federal government's Workforce Investment Act no longer allows the local Workforce Boards to directly deliver the education and training, community and technical colleges have often stepped in to become the primary source of workforce training in America.

Colleges and universities wanting to partner with business have new opportunities – the trend in corporate training is toward outsourcing this function – and institutions wanting to stay in the Ivory Tower may starve there.

Large, public universities help socialize immature students. They have refined choices to serve exceptionally bright and ambitious students. These institutions also have the capacity to offer a wide variety of academic programs and research that would not be possible at other types of institutions.[80] In short, they are important to us.

So is a liberal arts education. In fact, in the sense that "liberal arts" means a liberal sprinkling of lots of knowledge, it may ultimately prove to be the most relevant learning model. Roger Smith, former chairman and CEO of General Motors says (in *Educating Managers*) that "people trained in the liberal arts...learn to tolerate ambiguity and to bring order out of apparent confusion. They have the kind of sideways thinking and cross-classifying habit of mind that comes from learning, among other things, the many different ways of looking at literary works, social systems, chemical processes, or languages."

Research often housed on or near university campuses gives the U.S. a huge advantage in global competition.

Nations around the world can train their students in basic skills that will allow them to take some American manufacturing and high-tech jobs. But few of these societies invest the monies in research and development that America does. So long as we invest in research – new discoveries, new applications, new technologies – we are investing in America's standard of living and in the quality of American jobs.

For-profit institutions, once regarded as step-sisters to non-profits, have often led the way in on-site and on-line delivery of education. At a reasonable cost they have provided a very fine product, addressing needs often identified through marketing efforts aimed at linking student preparation to employer desires. While more high-brow institutions were disdainful of "job preparation" as a basis for curriculum, students in for-profit institutions were learning the competencies actually needed for career entrance and advancement.[81]

Higher education needs to become the wellspring for continuous learning. No single institution is responsible to manage America through the jobs revolution, which is part of the challenge. This is everyone's problem and, therefore, it belongs to no one. The challenges are spread across many institutions from churches to corporations, schools to political parties. We are rapidly becoming better at seeing the problems – from minority education to an aging workforce – but these are problems no one institution can solve.

Colleges and universities cannot do it alone either. But higher education, including graduate education, is uniquely positioned to forge new collaborations with private- and public-sector interest groups, on- and off-campus, on- and off-line.

Education must be seen not simply as a goal but, in a jobs revolution, as the most critical strategy. Learning should be recognized for what it is, a tool enabling us to work, to play, to dream and to live with greater security, broader satisfaction and better service. It is not an end in itself. It is the key strategy by which we can work and live with purpose and satisfaction throughout our lives. It equips us for employment, but it does more than that. It equips us to make a difference in the lives of others and, thereby, to enjoy a satisfaction that far exceeds a paycheck or a business card.

Chapter Nine

The Long View: Revolution in Context

The one factor that has had the biggest impact on the American workplace in recent decades is *productivity*. Farms produce vastly more per worker, per acre and per dollar than ever before. Manufacturing firms produce more products with fewer employees and the service sector increasingly provides more service without a corresponding growth in the number of workers.[82]

Increased productivity – meaning, more yield per dollar spent – is splendid and troubling. It means we are more efficient in producing goods and services. It also means we need fewer people to do the job.

In the short run, all the complicated strands woven through the jobs revolution have an edge of trouble in them. Productivity gains can mean fewer people on the line. Lower-cost employees in other nations can mean American jobs crossing borders. Global technologies that let us see our children fighting in Iraq also let engineers in India do the work previously done by engineers in Indianapolis. The creation of new jobs requiring new education may mean that older workers too frightened or too weary to return to school

In the short run all the complicated strands woven through the jobs revolution have an edge of trouble in them. In the long view, the jobs revolution is overwhelmingly positive.

opt out of the workforce just when worker shortages loom. Up close, every feature of this revolution has a down side. Ask someone in Greenville, Michigan, and they'll explain it to you.

Admitting all this, let us nonetheless offer a brief interlude in which we take the longer view. This requires that we stop, for a moment, looking at light bulbs as if we are candle makers, or cars as if we're carriage builders.

In the long view, the jobs revolution is overwhelmingly positive. As Alan Greenspan says, this is the way it's always been: "This process is not new. For generations American ingenuity has been creating industries and jobs that never existed before, from vehicle assemblers to computer software engineers." It's true. Bureau of Labor Statistics numbers show growth of jobs and income decade-after-decade: In 1959, there were 54,175,000 non-farm jobs and the median per capita income in the U.S. was $2,606 (which, given inflation, would equate to $15,578 in Year 2004 dollars). Every decade thereafter both numbers climbed until, in 1999, we had 130,536,000 non-farm jobs and a per-capita income of $23,344 (in "Year 2004 dollars").[83]

Harvard professor Joseph Schumpeter calls the creation and dissolution of jobs "creative destruction." Capital saved from disinvesting in outmoded, noncompetitive industries is reinvested in new processes and technologies. As always within these revolutions, workers able to migrate to new jobs have a sense of opportunity, growth and expectations for an increased standard of living.

Since 1929 the American economy has risen steadily, employment opportunities have mushroomed, wages and personal income have escalated and the standard of living in America has approached levels unimagined in human history (and in most of today's world). Progress was interrupted but never, long-term, reversed. U.S. Gross Domestic Production has continued to grow at average annual rates of 3.4 percent; employment has grown by an average of 1.5 percent; productivity has increased at the rate of 1.8 percent; per-capita personal income is up 50 percent in 40 years. The "creative destruction" of old jobs has, like the forest fire so essential to new growth, made way for needed jobs expansion. The fire itself is destructive; the growth that follows is redemptive.

In the decade spanning 1994 to 2004, America lost nearly 2.7 million manufacturing jobs, some to exporting and most to productivity gains. During the past ten years output per hour of work has increased 28 percent and overall factory efficiency has increased 47 percent.[84] Factories operating at twice the efficiency of just 10 years ago will simply not need the same number of workers to produce the same amount of product.

The quandary facing America is not whether we can save every job but whether we can replace outmoded jobs with others of equal or more value. The answer is, "Yes, we can."

The quandary facing America is not whether we can save every job but whether we can replace outmoded jobs with others of equal or more value. The answer is, "Yes, we can."

But two problems persist. First, and immediately, this cycle leaves growing numbers of jobless Americans who can't make it from outmoded to new jobs. Second, and not far in the future, we'll create wonderful new jobs without equipping enough Americans to fill them – thus, we'll create jobs that must go elsewhere. (Forrester Research now projects that, by 2015, 3.4 million "white collar" jobs going offshore at a cost of $100-150 billion annually.)

Americans, young or old, who invest in their education will have a terrific pay-off. Those unwilling or unable to make this investment face an America in which the number and range of lower-skill jobs rapidly declines, soon reaching the historic low of 12 percent new-job creation. So jobs that are disappearing require lower skills and jobs that are being created require higher skills. In the long run this exchange favors America, especially if we find ways to fill the higher-skill positions.

Massive workplace changes accompanying previous revolutions came at a slower clip than those arriving today. Throughout the industrial revolution, for example, the job market moved *between* generations: Parents stayed on the farm and children moved to the city. It was always "the next generation" that took on new jobs.

But newness arrives in our high-tech, global-economy world at an electric pace that leaves no time for pushing off change to the next generation. The next generation must be equipped to work in a very new economy. But focusing on the next generation is insufficient because much of the current workforce needs continued employment too. The rapidity with which changes are arriving makes us catch our breath. The jobs revolution may have a long-view, positive context. But it's hard to remember in a short-term unemployment line.

Jobs have become increasingly multi-skilled with a widened scope of responsibility; this means they are more interesting and, potentially, more satisfying. In the long run, productivity gains are measured not by job reductions but by increased output of the workforce that remains on the job. Rather than the old model of "high wages for low skills" the new workplace is characterized by "higher wages for higher skills." And all of this is good, positive, encouraging for the future and rewarding for most in the present.

Put another way: For those with higher skills, it's an exciting and rewarding workplace. For those without them, it's a nail-biting time.

America, among the family of nations, controls most of the global and technical forces of change. What we have not yet done is harness those forces to sound policy that will stimulate the investment needed to build the workforce of tomorrow.

The way America works has changed dramatically. Children seldom take their parents' jobs in today's workforce. Technology and the demand for new skills have redefined the role and value of the American worker, and the process of redefinition has only just begun. The Internet is changing where we work, when we work, how we work and even whether we work. Individual workers enjoy greater flexibility, more freedom and finer rewards than a turn-of-the-century trade unionist could have imagined possible. This is the long view of the jobs revolution at the beginning of the 21st Century, what we see when we look up and out.

The jobs revolution may have a long-view, positive context. But it's hard to remember in a short-term unemployment line.

But when we look down and around ourselves today, we see casualties of the revolution. To assure that the jobs revolution really *does* have a positive outcome, we must rely not on historical trends but on real decisions made with urgency and collaboration by America's leaders, and soon.

Living through the jobs revolution can be like going around inside a cement mixer where it's hard to recall that the original goal was a long, smooth driveway. The positive view is important because it reminds us that the opportunities are real – and that we need to go get them.

Chapter Ten

What's a Community To Do?

No one is rolling up the sidewalks of Greenville, Michigan. The community is proving resilient. In the wake of the hard news that the town's largest employer is leaving, leaders from both the public and the private sector are rallying the citizenry. And Greenville is not alone.

Iowa Governor Tom Vilsack tells this story:

> *About a one-hour drive east of the Iowa-Illinois border is a town called Galesburg, Illinois. It's a community like many in this country. There are churches, schools, and grocery stores. And like communities around the country, families in Galesburg are suffering because of massive manufacturing job losses.*
>
> *Maytag's refrigerator plant shut down and shifted its operations to Mexico. As a result, lawmakers in Illinois think the unemployment rate in Galesburg could soar as high as 25 percent. 1,600 jobs have been lost already, and Western Illinois University is projecting that the region eventually may lose more than 4,100 jobs because of the Maytag closure.*
>
> *I heard a man from Galesburg named Jim McGovern Jr. interviewed on the news one night. In the report, Mr. McGovern said that although he had managed to keep his job at Maytag, his wife had lost hers. She*

had found new work in Michigan and Mr. McGovern was driving every other weekend to visit her. Mr. McGovern then learned that his reserve unit has been called up for duty in Iraq.

The reporter asked him what concerned him more: going to Iraq or trying to find a new job. Mr. McGovern answered that he worried more about having to find a new job.[85]

Another quiet community in another Midwestern state, another refrigerator manufacturer heading south. Maytag left Galesburg for approximately the same reasons Electrolux left Greenville.

There are enough available ideas and models to enable most communities to emerge grateful for the jobs revolution. Being proactive, while it sounds prosaic, is critical.

Exported jobs is only one job-revolution challenge, and not the most significant. But it's famous for two reasons. First, one person losing her job is a shame but not a headline. A plant closing is a front-page story in almost any community. Second, exported jobs is a political hot button used as a wedge issue in campaigns. It makes a great sound bite.

Mostly, the jobs revolution is not a headline-making event. In most communities it's a quiet revolution impacting us one employee, one family, one job at a time. When you add up all the "ones" you have millions, but the one-at-a-time phenomenon keeps the story in the closet. The American economy may be rebounding but if you are a working single mother who left high school before graduation to care for a child, you are almost certain to be "one." If you're a 40-year-old with a perfect, 20-year work record at your local tool-and-die shop, but with no advanced training and no computer skills, the jobs revolution is looking for you; you're "one." Fifty-year-olds hoping to slide into retirement; 60-year-olds wanting to hang onto benefits and pensions – "sliding" and "hanging on" are dangerous verbs, predictors that someone is about to become "one."

So what's a community to do if it wants to be a workers' and employers' haven during a jobs revolution?

At its core, the jobs revolution tests our community values. Where communities value education enough to build and maintain strong schools, promote open and full admission for all youth (especially minorities), encourage employed and non-employed adults to continue their own education, and tie education and training to economic development – these values will see a community through the jobs revolution.

Communities that genuinely value their economic base will also value their workforce. How do we "value" employers? By engaging them in surveys and conversations about their workforce needs; by determining whether they are satisfied with the workforce available in the community; by inviting, even cajoling, them into collaborative efforts to measure, plan and sponsor the strongest possible community workforce. The nation's Workforce Investment Act was written to bring local business leaders into the design and delivery of education and training programs in their community. Business leaders need to be community leaders, and step up to the plate in workforce development.

If we wait for headlines and crises, it is almost certain to be too late to prevent the economic havoc faced by a Galesburg or a Greenville. These communities are rallying but they are doing it in the face of huge challenges. Each of them would wish the crisis had never occurred. But if we are genuinely passionate about building an all-inclusive, community-based workforce as the platform for economic development, there are enough available ideas and models to enable most communities to emerge grateful for the jobs revolution. Being proactive, while it sounds prosaic, is critical.

The most effective workforce is one that welcomes people no matter their age, gender, ethnicity or religion. It meets the community's need for low-paying, lower-skill positions (often, the stepping stones for young people to gain their first work experience), for higher-paying, high-skill posts, and for a full range of professional options. Young people are valued not only as customers or clients or patients but also as guests, learners and interns. Adults returning to the workforce after years of absence are greeted with patience and appreciation for the life skills they've mastered, even if computer technology demands new learning. Every person who wants to work is seen as a community resource, an essential economic resource. Quite simply, it is a recognition that human capital – not machinery – is the greatest resource of our economic future.

A community with leaders who worry about the future of their workforce, and act on that worry with sound analysis, planning and collaboration, is a community unlikely to be hurt by the jobs revolution.

At a community level, the jobs revolution is about valuing students. The clearest evidence of such valuing may be the federal legislation, *No Child Left Behind.* Questions of implementation and funding aside – and we do understand their importance – this legislation is historic for various reasons, including its bipartisan support.

First, it represents the most dramatic expansion of the federal role in K-12 education ever. It emerged from a legislative recognition of life in the global economy. When America began public education, we were a nation of farm and small-town families that never left home.

That's not life in America today; this legislation confirms the need for change.

Second, this legislation recognizes the urgency of providing all children, especially our minority and low-income students, with equal education opportunities and outcomes. We know that today's students are tomorrow's workers, or they'll be tomorrow's unemployed. In initial assessments, we've discovered that not all students are getting equal education; minorities suffer. The question is, What will we do about it?

We need communities that value their children enough to link education and economics, today's classroom with tomorrow's boardroom. When communities are committed, the workforce is being prepared – and it's happening most of all in the community's schools.

At a community level, the jobs revolution is about valuing workers. What's true of children in the educational system is increasingly true of workers in training programs.

The old concept of workforce training as "a second-chance system" is being rapidly replaced by a model of workforce training as economic development. Those workers who've fallen through employment cracks may still need a second, third or fourth chance. But the purpose of most regional workforce development programs is moving from a model of social and employment rehabilitation to a model of economic benefit for employees and employers. Workforce development is becoming less of a rescue mission and more of an investment program. By its very mission, the Workforce Investment Act must now provide "universal access" to all residents – the

No single institution is responsible to manage America through the jobs revolution, which is part of the challenge.

un-employed, the under-employed, and the employed seeking new skills.

New trends are emerging. Employer-recognized certification, growing alignments with educational outcomes, expanding regional partnerships with industries and academic institutions, and increased use of technology and on-line education are found almost everywhere. Those programs that win community support have proven the ability to "graduate" participants with formal, employer-recognized credentials as well as a high school diploma or GED (employer-recognized certification awards increased 156 percent between 1990 and 1998, and have continued to escalate).[86]

The relationship between the employer and the learning participant is critical. When employers demonstrate that their workers are genuinely valued, valued enough to have the company invest thousands of dollars in their learning, everyone wins: employees, employers and communities.

If community and technical colleges were once viewed as second-class citizens in the higher education kingdom, that view is gone. So important are these colleges to community economies that in nearly every region they have become an organizing partner in economic development and the delivery vehicle for workforce training.

The preeminence of community colleges is fascinating. At most four-year colleges, adult workers who return for education are called "non-traditional students." The term itself tells the story: These aren't the students for whom this institution is built. By comparison (and despite the community-college image of recruiting mainly high school seniors), half of community college students are 25 years or older and a third are 30 or older.[87] The average community college student is

29.[88] A suburban Chicago campus, Oakton Community College, regularly hosts a student body in which 40 percent have previously earned four-year degrees,[89] and "degreed, returning" students are commonplace on most community college campuses.

When the Workforce Investment Act was amended so that Workforce Investment Boards could no longer engage directly in the delivery of services, this responsibility moved mostly to community and technical colleges, thus giving these institutions a further boost. As a consequence, demand for admission to these schools has led to 2003 headlines like that of the *Orlando* (FL) *Sentinel*: "Community Colleges Turn Away 35,000." The *Sentinel* observed that enrollments in Florida were already up 5.8 percent; even so, demand outstripped capacity by at least "35,000 students hoping to enroll."[90]

Workforce development is becoming less of a rescue mission and more of an investment program.

The rise of community and technical colleges in the preparation of America's workforce may be the most under-reported story in education today. America has some 1,171 public, private and tribal institutions providing job preparation at more than 1,600 campuses serving in excess of 11.6 million students annually.[91] This represents just under half (44 percent) of all students enrolled in postsecondary education in America.

And the demographics of community and technical colleges are stunning. They lead the nation in serving growing minority populations with 47 percent of Black undergraduate students, 56 percent of Hispanic undergraduates, 48 percent of Asian undergraduates and 57 percent of Native American undergraduates.[92] No other source of higher education is even close to meeting the needs of these populations at the pace of community colleges. Some community colleges are still too focused on semester courses and student loan re-imbursement to respond wisely to new opportunities. But the number of such schools is dropping, often at the demand of business and community leadership.

Communities can wait for crises or plan for success. We can sit on the track and get run over, or we can move. We can wait for something to go wrong, or we can make sure it doesn't.

The outline of the jobs revolution is patently clear. It emerges from a growing, global economy shaping an American workforce that increasingly values high-skilled employees. Because we will face shortages of workers and skills in the U.S. within about five years, we cannot waste any human resources. Most communities must improve our ability to adequately prepare and employ minorities and youth. The half-life of formal education is shrinking while the demand for continuous learning and retraining is escalating. And we can draw a big, fat, straight line between education and employment. If our community schools are superior, our workforce will be better and our economic future will be stronger. This is not a guess; it's a fact.

Development of a comprehensive national policy for workforce development is imperative. We must begin by recognizing that effective education has become a right, not merely an opportunity.

Every major workforce trend needed to form effective community plans has been identified and catalogued. The jobs revolution is quiet but it is not mysterious. We can understand its dynamics and change its outcomes. The choices are ours.

We need to think resources and think reform. We will need an additional public investment in education and training. (To suggest less would be dishonest.) We'll need reform of higher education's student grant and loan eligibility rules to accommodate adult, non-traditional, part-time students. We surely need more flexibility in the design and delivery of our educational curricula.

Most of all, we need leaders of the private sector – from business to philanthropy, agriculture to healthcare – to join with leaders from the public sector to meet workforce needs. This is not "government's job" or "the private-sector's job." It is our job to ensure jobs in every American community.

Chapter Eleven

In Need of a Champion

One of the most amazing political stories of the past decade has been the lack of interest in America's workforce. Suddenly, in the past few months, the story has broken everywhere under banner headlines screaming about jobs.

How this crept up on us is uncertain. Chronic unemployment of 6 percent would normally create a major political issue but the highest unemployment numbers in nine years had no discernible impact on the 2002 and 2004 elections. Cuts in federal investment in job training should raise alarms beyond the training professionals; it hasn't. Youth unemployment especially in minority communities is a scandal; the media doesn't mention it. No major business organization made workforce investment key to their legislative agenda. Only recently have American leaders apparently sensed the impact and the opportunity the jobs revolution is having on America's workforce.

Never before in American history has the economic success of our minorities been as important to the majority population as it is now and will be in the next decade.

Now that jobs have the attention of national leaders, someone needs to help us past rhetoric and sound bites to solid plans and reasonable action.

Development of a comprehensive national policy for workforce development is imperative. We must begin by recognizing that effective education has become a right, not merely an opportunity. It is the basis for every American's security and professional growth.

Reality: We are a nation at risk. But our young and our working adults are stunningly ill-prepared, and lack of preparation compounds challenges of diversity: 84 percent of White workers, 91 percent of Black and 97 percent of Hispanic workers entered today's workforce *without* college degrees. The educational challenge to keep these individuals competitive is breathtaking. See who's coming to work between now and the year 2010: Whites will increase 9 percent, Blacks 21 percent, Hispanics and Asians by 43 percent – most workers coming from ethnic groups that are most educationally challenged. No wonder Cisco Systems complained that 39 percent of its current workforce and 26 percent of new hires suffer basic skill deficiencies. Overlay all this with increased skill demands to compete globally, and there's one conclusion: We are at risk.

The challenge of paying for two generations in retirement while educating and training their replacements is probably America's greatest fiscal challenge.

Reality: Building a diverse and a successful workforce is a requirement, not an option. We know the knowledge and skill requirements in America's future workplace, and we know the increased diversity in that workplace. Blacks, Asians and Hispanics in America will increase their population over the next decade at rates four to five times greater than the White majority.[93]

Guaranteeing the success of minority workers should appeal not only to the moral standards of American communities but also to the selfish interests of each American. Unless we are able to educate, train, place and appropriately compensate our growing minority workers, we will not be able to sustain the Social Security and Medicare benefits for the Grandpa and Grandma Olsons living in the nation's heartland. Never before in American history has the economic success of our minorities been as important to the majority population as it is now and will be in the next decade.

Reality: We are at the edge of a massive pension and entitlement crisis. 76 million baby boomers will retire while only 46 million "Generation Xers" enter the workforce.[94] This math won't work. Left unsolved, it will rob needed resources from essential education and training investments.

In 1951, the average American worker lived 11 years in retirement. Today's average retiree enjoys 18 years of retirement. Everyone wants longer life and no one wants to pay for it. Thus, in 2004, the Pension Benefit Guarantee Corporation reached a record deficit of $23.3 billion. Congress recently responded to the concerns of senior citizen drug costs by enacting a $400 - 500 billion Prescription Drug Program. We project annual deficits in the federal budget of between $250 and $350 billion in the next few years. It's unworkable math.

The challenge of paying for two generations in retirement while educating and training their replacements is probably America's greatest fiscal challenge.

Reality: We need new models of learning. Other nations have focused on improved educational outcomes, more expansive access to technology and better financial support for students. When they do this, they pass us as if we're standing still. The average U.S. student begins on top of the world in math and science in elementary school, but by the 12th grade, overall U.S. student performance has sunk to near the bottom of international comparisons, with low income and minority students faring the worst. As a result, effective education has become a "right" not merely an opportunity.

How can we hope for a strong economy when 60 percent of new U.S. jobs require skills possessed by only 22 percent of young Americans currently entering the job market?

America's richest source of new workers is minority youth. Today, somewhere between 25 and 30 percent of America's teenagers, including recent immigrants, fail to graduate from high school.[95] In the decade of the '90s dropouts ranged from a low of 380,000 to a high of 604,000 and we've seen average dropouts of over 500,000 in the past five years.[96] Combined with the disturbing youth unemployment rates almost three times the national average for all workers, we have a recipe for workforce disaster. Unions running apprenticeship programs, schools engaging in distance education and community-based organizations providing intensive training are all part of a new, diverse, customer-friendly delivery system. Perhaps these can save us, or at least stem the tide, provided they meet the standards of educational quality and performance outcomes.

America's competitiveness in the high-tech, global economy is guided by labor law last reformed in the 1950s when Detroit sold cars by adding chrome, not value.

Reality: We need a comprehensive system of human resource development in America that reflects the emerging needs. Without a boatload of mandates and federal controls, we must better integrate the scatter of education and training programs. Basic education must be tied to emerging careers. Job training can no longer be limited to disadvantaged and displaced workers. Nearly half of today's enrolled students are "non-traditional" adult learners, but student financial aid programs barely reach this population. Standards for accreditation are outmoded. Support for private initiatives is divided between literally dozens of federal offices and agencies. Tossed salads have more internal cohesion than the federal policy on human resource development.

Reality: We must support individuals who've lost jobs and need assistance to gain new skills. Those displaced by the jobs revolution need an opportunity to return to the workforce. We cannot afford, morally or economically, to lose human resources when our nation is about to suffer a shortage of workers and unfilled jobs are sure to leave the country.

Unemployment insurance (UI) was designed in the labor market of the past. Companies, jobs and skills were stable and UI was only intended to provide short-term assistance during temporary corporate or economic downturns, not as a bridge to new skills and new jobs.

> *Mostly, the jobs revolution is not a headline-making event. In most communities it's a quiet revolution impacting us one employee, one family, one job at a time. When you add up all the "ones" you have millions, but the one-at-a-time phenomenon keeps the story in the closet.*

In 2003 states spent over $42 billion on unemployment compensation. But such assistance without parallel training and education assistance is a cruel hoax on the worker, the community and the economy. We should seriously consider transferring such a commitment into "employment insurance" with an educational component.

Americans pay for health insurance, car insurance, life insurance, even pet insurance. It's time to consider wage insurance as a means of protecting and assisting workers in the rapid change of the workforce revolution. If we add the $56 billion paid by employers for in-house training to the $42 billion we pay to people not to work, we'd have more than $100 billion with which to keep people employed – insuring America's competitive future.

It takes a long time to get Federal legislation, and longer to get rid of it. Most of the laws and regulations overseeing America's workforce were developed for a different world, many during the industrial revolution. America's competitiveness in the high-tech, global economy is guided by labor law last reformed in the 1950s when Detroit sold cars by adding chrome, not value.

The federal government is a sluggish behemoth that creeps and crawls, except in times of emergency. In crises, it can respond amazingly well. Rules are shelved and constraints are lifted; speed becomes the order of the day. But during a quiet transformation like the jobs revolution, federal policy involves vast pondering and plodding.

The two big challenges at a federal-policy level are pace, which is brutally slow, and clumsiness resulting from lack of coordination between the legislative and executive branches.

What's lacking is not only legislation but leadership. Someone needs to help break down barriers to economic responsiveness. Someone needs to champion the government's rightful role, lead the government's engagement with the private sector, coordinate federal responses through the canyons and gullies of the bureaucracy. We are, after all, putting billions of dollars into various programs within sight of the jobs revolution. That, if nothing else, should matter.

The Comprehensive Employment and Training Act (CETA) in the 1970s sought to make individuals employable, whether the workplace needed their skills or not. The 1980s Job Training Partnership Act bolstered state and local control to improve alignment of training and real employment needs in each region. In 1998 the Workforce Investment Act made employment training more accessible and comprehensive, encouraging efficiency through "one-stop centers" and greater business leadership in program design. But all this took 30 years and, in today's global market, is woefully inadequate.

The two big challenges at a federal-policy level are *pace*, which is brutally slow, and *clumsiness* resulting from lack of coordination between the legislative and executive branches.

Policy is slowed because we are a nation divided evenly between Republicans and Democrats, rendering it nearly impossible to develop a consensus on human resource issues. It took 20 years to transplant ideas from the publication *A Nation at Risk* into passage of *No Child Left Behind*. More Americans are without health insurance today than when the Clintons first proposed their program in 1993. School-to-work transition programs and Youth Opportunity Grants, both programs targeting those most at risk, have fallen victim to the partisan divisions in politics today.

While the policy side of government seems paralyzed, the executive branch is more consumed with protecting turf than solving problems. Secretary of Health and Human Services Tommy Thompson gave a blistering summary of how one navigates our nation's federal bureaucracy.

> *You have to vet an idea through as many as 12 divisions with 63,000 employees before you can move it forward to get consensus and, after that, it goes to the Office of Management and Budget. They turn you down nine times out of ten—because they can, and because they want to show you who the boss is. If it gets by them, it goes to the President.*

> *If it gets the President's support, it goes on to Congress, and if they ever pass it, it's probably about time for you to retire. That's why there is so much inertia in the federal government to retain the status quo.*[97]

While we dawdle at a federal level, other nations are moving – sprinting – forward. Samuel Palmisano, President of IBM, observed it closely:

> *Based on a study that IBM commissioned, the 42 industries represented by the Council on Competitiveness will create 13 million jobs worldwide over the next two years and more than 95 million jobs over the next decade. The question is where those jobs will be. Job creation, like innovation, can occur almost anywhere. China, India, South Korea, and other nations are replicating the structural advantages that have made the U.S. the center of innovation. These nations are becoming very competitive, and it would be naïve to believe that phenomenon is based solely on wages. They are investing in education and job skills; teaching their citizens the languages of modern commerce (English, software, genomics, and finance); and building modern network infrastructures.*[98]

Leadership for a comprehensive strategy should rise at the federal level because it is here that all the components of the strategy, and all the participants, can be gathered: youth and adults, experts in employment and labor, private sector leaders and public servants.

Jeffrey E. Garten, Dean of Yale's School of Management, believes the day of reckoning is coming. "I don't see anything on the near-term horizon showing that our political or business leaders see the problem in its proper dimensions," he wrote. "But if my concerns are only half right, it won't be too long before they'll have to."[99] In other words, he believes our leaders will do the right thing when all other options have been exhausted.

We need a federal workforce development policy built on the model of great return on investment. The most important federal program in job training is the Higher Education Act, not the Workforce Investment Act.

Today, the federal government spends over $17 billion on higher education programs, $3.3 billion on workforce training, and $2.1 billion on vocational education. We spend less educating Americans to work than we do paying for them to be out of work – a system liked by neither the unemployed nor the taxpayer.

The Workforce Investment Act of 1998 implies a commitment to serve the nation's workforce, but its real focus is on those who have fallen out of the workforce. It's an important program for those it serves but lacks a proactive reach, adequate resources and the engagement of business needed to actually deliver employment skills to workers and potential workers in all communities, thus stopping the flow of new casualties.

No trade agreements and no investment in unemployment insurance will alter the reality that productivity gains mean job losses. What we need to do is invest in those still working, before they are displaced....

A sound, comprehensive, proactive policy would start with an economic model that we can compete globally only when we (1) provide an education that prepares all students with the requisite skills levels for 21st Century jobs, (2) deliver technical education based on employer recognized certification to ensure employment relevance and (3) create *employment* insurance to assure access to skill training for those caught in the transition.

Throughout American history we have witnessed an expanding economy, and a growth in both the number and the quality of jobs available. This is, as Alan Greenspan says, "the unique American experience."[100] We should examine this experience and, seeing the vast number of employed Americans, ask, "How will we keep them employed?" This doesn't mean we ignore those suffering unemployment, any more than focusing on good health means we won't treat cancer. Productivity gains alone demand some response. We needed 18.9 million manufacturing workers to produce $888 billion worth of manufactured goods in 1987; by 2000, we were producing nearly twice as much with 500,000 less workers. No trade agreements and no investment in *un*employment insurance will alter the reality that productivity gains mean job losses.[101] What we need to do is invest in those still working, before they are displaced – and we can tell who these people are, what they are doing and what their needs are.

As a nation we are investing, arguably, $5 billion to enable people to stay at work and $42 billion when they do not.

Our economy will grow. Most economists anticipate an improved GDP, up around 4 percent. Average wages will see a small raise, in the 3-4 percent range. If manufacturing jobs trended downward, manufacturing output remains strong (the Federal Reserve recorded the largest monthly gain in manufacturing since 1999 in late 2003).[102] And American innovation is thriving: over 350,000 patent registrations were filed with the United States Patent Office in 2002.[103] Global markets, in general, remain our friends. China hopes to create eight million new jobs in 2004 and we hope to sell goods to all of them as we count down to the 2008 Olympic Games. General Motors plans to produce almost 100,000 cars in Russia by 2005.[104] Every one of these items should matter to American workforce policy.

The federal government has, since 2001, unleashed the largest increase in K-12 education funding in history. President Clinton's final budget contained $24.8 billion for this cause; $38.5 billion is the number in President Bush's 2006 budget submission to Congress, a whopping 55 percent increase in federal funding, $13.7 billion in five years. But at the same time, funding for our nation's Workforce Investment Programs has actually *decreased* from $3.7 billion in Fiscal Year 2000 to $3.4 billion in Fiscal Year 2005.

A comprehensive, investment-based U.S. policy on workforce development urgently needs private as well as public funds and leadership. But it's reasonable to believe that the policy itself should rise from our nation's governing leaders. They, like all of us, may suffer when all the statistics and numbers become a blur. But someone should hold on, and plan from, just these few bits of data:

- In 2004 the federal government invested some $17 billion in higher education, much of it in the form of financial aid to which most American workers have no access;
- We invested about $3.3 billion in job training and $2.1 billion in vocational education, programs intended to promote workforce development; and
- We paid a staggering $43 billion to help people stay out of work in a program called "unemployment."

Those out of work deserve sympathy, support and another chance. Don't misunderstand us. But as a nation we are investing, arguably, $5.4 billion to enable people to stay at work and $43 billion when they do not.

As our teenaged friends would say, "What's wrong with this picture – duh?"

Chapter Twelve

Training Chauffeurs

The manuscript for *The Jobs Revolution* was being edited between our various offices when Kathryn Scanland answered the phone in her Chicago office. One of Dr. Scanland's tasks is to direct Greystone's research. Someone doing a search of the corporate web site had spotted her name.

"In perfect English," Kathryn noted, "a recorded voice offered to do telephone support for our research. The voicemail messenger, speaking in flawless English, was very upfront about the fact that he was calling from India where the work would also be done." Kathryn's caller assumed we would know that telephone polling done from India is cheaper than that conducted from Chicago.

The same week Alan Greenspan spoke in Omaha, Nebraska. He understood why fears about unemployment are so high in the U.S. when "nearly two million of our workforce have been unemployed for more than a year." He tried to give an historical perspective.

> *Those who have lost jobs, I know, are not readily consoled by the fact that current job insecurity concerns are not new. But keeping the current period in context is instructive. Jobs in the United States were perceived as migrating to low-wage Japan in the 1950s and 1960s, to low-wage Mexico in the 1990s, and most recently to low-wage China. ...Many in Mexico are now complaining of job losses to low-wage China.*

> *...The loss of jobs over the past three years is attributable largely to rapid declines in the demand for industrial goods and to outsized gains in productivity that have caused effective supply to outstrip demand. Protectionism will do little to create jobs, and if foreigners retaliate we will surely lose jobs. We need instead to discover the means to enhance the skills of our workforce and to further open markets here and abroad to allow our workers to compete effectively in the global marketplace.*

In the days following Mr. Greenspan's insightful analysis, with which we heartily agree, we heard no thundering response from Capital Hill or America's business community. Eight million people unemployed did not rally a cry of urgency or a demand for change until the presidential campaigns got fully underway. Then, "jobs" became more of a weapon of attack than an object of thoughtful analysis.

What Mr. Greenspan and others need to know, we offer respectfully, is that the "means to enhance the skills of our workforce" need not be discovered; they already have been. What we lack is not knowledge of the means but adequate national leadership and the will to act on what we know.

Every policy is built on a platform of assumptions. Norman Macrae (in *The Economist*) reminded us of the Mercedes Corporation survey in 1903 to learn the marketplace limits for production of automobiles. Mercedes wanted to know how many cars they could reasonably expect to sell. The study brilliantly demonstrated that Mercedes could never sell more than one million cars. The rationale? There would never be more than one million men trainable as chauffeurs.

Assumptions matter. If we assume that there are too few jobs and too many workers, we are looking backward, not forward. We need to prepare for an American jobs market in which there are too many openings and not enough skilled workers to fill them. When this happens, American jobs will leave the country at exponential rates. Unless we act now.

If we assume that the demographics of today's workforce will also be the face of tomorrow's, we set off on the wrong foot. Minorities and youth are the people we must reach, motivate, equip and continuously educate. They are our hope for a competitive workforce.

If we assume that hard work and a completed education will carry us through our careers, we're mistaken. We will need continually buffed-up skills based on constantly refreshed learning. As long as we want to work we will need to learn.

And if we assume that the federal government will lead the way to a better workforce tomorrow,

What we lack is not knowledge...but adequate national leadership and the will to act on what we know.

we are expecting miracles not yet demonstrated by saints in Washington, D.C. The jobs revolution is sweeping America while the urgency to change priorities, from funding *unemployment* to funding *employment*, goes wonting.

Action matters. The jobs revolution is an historic, social, economic and political reality. In places like Greenville, Michigan, and Galesburg, Illinois, it's easy to find people who will believe it. In places where catastrophe has not yet struck and employees are becoming un-employees one-at-a-time, it's a hard sell.

We can make the case with statistics, as we've tried in this book, hoping to draw a paint-by-number picture of America's workforce needs and possibilities. Frankly, we did it holding our breath, remembering Darrell Huff's wonderful essay ("How to Lie with Statistics") in which he argued that "Americans use statistics like drunks use lamp posts, for support instead of illumination."

While we wrote, the statistics moved, almost never in a happier direction. *The Investor's Business Daily* (March 8, 2004) posted the latest news under a headline reading "Job Growth Shriveled Up In Feb."

After a speech given by Steve Gunderson a veteran educator – Sandra Ericson – wrote about her perspective at City College in San Francisco where for 15 years she has equipped people to enter and stay in the workforce. Her thoughtful concern was that "focusing on the development of our future workforce solely in terms of occupational skills misses half the problem: The other half is how to prepare people to be self-sufficient." As she rightly concluded: "Existing still comes before working."

Minorities and youth are the people we must reach, motivate, equip and continuously educate. They are our hope for a competitive workforce.

The Washington Post (March 4, 2004) urged presidential candidates and others to go beyond sound bites to sound policy, inviting leading politicians to "think big about the job market. They should struggle to improve public education. They should invest more in retraining for laid-off workers. They should minimize taxes that directly penalize job creation...." Wise counsel that has, at this writing, thus far yielded no obvious action.

The saddest statistic may be the number of Americans who just stopped looking for work. The January 2004 Bureau of Labor Statistics report indicated that the U.S. unemployment rate went down from 5.9 to 5.7 percent. On the face of it, that seems like good news. But the companion item that explains this statistic is that 309,000 Americans voluntarily gave up searching for employment. In February, another 392,000 checked out of the system. Nearly three-quarters of a million Americans simply quit.[105]

We are growing desperate for leaders who will go beyond speeches to action. America has four, maybe six, years in which to radically revamp its fundamental assumptions about workforce development and then to act. Whatever is going to be done to prepare us for shortages of workers and skills, increased global competition, disparities in achievement between ethnic American communities and technology that changes while we sleep – whatever we are going to do, must be done now.

All that is at stake is our children. And our communities. And our future.

Endnotes

[1] Easterbrook, G. 2003. *The progress paradox: How life gets better while people feel worse*, New York: Random House, p. 64.
[2] Ibid. p. 65.
[3] Uhalde, R. 2005. Personal correspondence to the author.
[4] Cooper, J., & Madigan, K. 2003. U.S.: A temporary reprieve for manufacturing, *Business Week*, September 29.
[5] Oxford Dictionary & Thesaurus. 1997. Oxford, England: Oxford University Press.
[6] Wildemeersch, D., Finger, M., & Jansen, T. 2000. *Adult education and social responsibility,* New York: Peter Lang.
[7] Jacques, R. 1996. *Manufacturing the employee: Management knowledge from the 19th to 21st centuries,* Thousand Oaks, CA: SAGE Publications.
[8] National Center for Education Statistics, http://nces.ed.gov/nall/historicaldata/litenroll.asp.
[9] Jacques, R. 1996. *Manufacturing the employee: Management knowledge from the 19th to 21st centuries,* Thousand Oaks, CA: SAGE Publications.
[10] Anderson, C. *The two centuries that invented the industrial revolution*, http://www.darex.com/indurevo.htm.
[11] Beard, C. & Beard M. 1944. *The Beards' basic history of the United States*, New York: Doubleday, Doran & Company, pp. 195.
[12] Jorgenson, D. 2001. *American economic growth in the information age*, an address presented to PFF's Aspen Summit.
[13] White House Office of the Press Secretary. 2000. *America's agenda for the information age*, March 3, 2000.
[14] Maehl, W. 2000. *Lifelong learning at its best: Innovative practices in adult credit programs,* San Francisco: Jossey-Bass.
[15] Donaldson, J. F., & Ross-Gordon, J. M. 1992. Population diversity and the organization and function of continuing higher education. In A. W. Lerner & B. K. King (Eds.), *Continuing higher education: The coming wave,* New York: Teachers College Press.
[16] Ibid.
[17] Drucker, P. 2001. *The essential Drucker,* New York: HarperCollins, p. 289.

[18] Boeckmann, B. 2003. Personal correspondence to author.
[19] Dorrer, J. 2003. Personal correspondence to author.
[20] Naisbitt, J. 1998. Presentation at the U.S.-Japan Committee meetings of the Center for Strategic & International Studies in Kyoto, Japan.
[21] Uhalde, R. 2003. National Center on Education and the Economy, in a speech to the National Governor's Association Workforce Development Forum, December 3.
[22] Max, A. 1999. Novel plan makes inroads against illiteracy in India's heartland, *The San Francisco Chronicle/Examiner*, February 28.
[23] Heilig, G.K. 1999. *ChinaFood. Can China feed itself?* IIASA,www.iiasa.ac.at/Research/LUCChinaFood/data/pop/pop_7.htm.
[24] Kinetz, E. 2003. Stephen Roach, Managing Director and Chief Economist of Morgan Stanley, in a round-table discussion, Who Wins and Who Loses as Jobs Move Overseas?, *The New York Times*, December 7.
[25] Flynn, L. 2003. New economy: Learning lessons about overseas support, *The New York Times*, December 8.
[26] Uhalde, R. 2003. National Center on Education and the Economy, Remarks presented to the National Governors Association Workforce Development Conference, December 3.
[27] Bureau of Economic Analysis, *U.S. International Trade in Goods and Services*, June 2004.
[28] Clinton, B. 1999. *A national dialogue on jobs and trade*, November 10.
[29] Zhao, J., & Guo, J. 2002. The restructuring of China's higher education: An experience for market economy and knowledge economy, *Educational Philosophy and Theory*, 34, 2.
[30] Kinetz, E. 2003. Stephen Roach, Managing Director and Chief Economist of Morgan Stanley, in a round-table discussion, Who Wins and Who Loses as Jobs Move Overseas?, *The New York Times*, December 7.
[31] Bureau of Labor Statistics. 2000.
[32] Uhalde, R. 2003. *High skills and low wages*, a presentation to the 2003 NGA Workforce Development Policy forum, December 3.
[33] Carnevale, A., NAM White Paper, Reported in Business 2.com.

[34] National Association of Manufacturing, *The skills gap, 2001.*
[35] Carnevale, A., & Fry, R. 2000. *Crossing the great divide*, Educational Testing Services.
[36] Bureau of Labor Statistics. 2003. Unemployment by Level of Education, August.
[37] http://pubdb3.census.gov/macro/032004/perinc/new03_001.htm.
[38] Braswell, J. 2001. *The nation's report card: Mathematics 2000*, U.S. Department of Education, National Center for Education Statistics, August.
[39] Perlstein, L. 2004. Report disputes U.S. high school graduation rates, *The Washington Post*, February 26.
[40] SallieMae. 2003. *High school dropout rate for men by ethnicity*, Chart I.3.
[41] SallieMae. 2003. *Enrollment rates by ethnicity*, Chart II.4.
[42] SallieMae. 2003. *Fall enrollment, by ethnicity/race*, Chart II.2.
[43] Smith, P. 2003. *The learning curve*, Chapter Two.
[44] *Chronicle of Higher Education.* 2003. Academe's Hispanic future, L, 14, November 28.
[45] U.S. Census Bureau. http://www.census.gov/population/projections/nations/summary.
[46] Agbo, S. 2000. Heterogeneity of the student body and meaning of "non-traditional" in US higher education. In H. G. Schuetze & M. Slowey (Eds.), *Higher education and lifelong learners: International perspectives on change* (pp. 149-169), New York: RoutledgeFalmer.
[47] U.S. Census Bureau. 2002. *Population projections.* http://www.census.gov/population/www/projections/popproj.html.
[48] Donaldson, J. F., & Ross-Gordon, J. M. 1992. Population diversity and the organization and function of continuing higher education. In A. W. Lerner & B. K. King (Eds.), *Continuing higher education: The coming wave,* New York: Teachers College Press.
[49] Drucker, P. F. 1998. The coming of the new organization. *Harvard business review on knowledge management* (pp.1-19), Boston, MA: Harvard Business School Publishing.
[50] Donaldson, J. F., & Ross-Gordon, J. M. 1992. Population diversity and the organization and function of continuing higher education. In A. W. Lerner & B. K. King (Eds.), *Continuing higher education: The coming wave,* New York: Teachers College Press.
[51] SallieMae. 2003. *High school dropout rate by gender*, Chart I.2.

[52] National Center for Education Statistics, *Digest of Education Statistics*, 2003.
[53] Ibid.
[54] Northeastern University. 2002. *The absent male worker and limited growth in New England's labor force in the 1990*, July.
[55] Greenspan, A. 2003. Remarks before the World Affairs Council of Greater Dallas, December 11.
[56] Uhalde, R. 2003. *Do Skills Still Matter in a Global Economy?*, presented at 2003 NGA Workforce Development Policy Forum, December 3.
[57] Ibid.
[58] Maynard, M. 2003. Interview in *The Christian Science Monitor*, October 15.
[59] The Globe and Mail. 2003. *Global auto sales growth in 2004*, December 30, http://www.globeandmail.com.
[60] Federal Reserve Bank of Dallas. 2003. *China, awakening giant*, F, September/October.
[61] Greenberg, E., & Grunberg, L. 2003. *The Changing American workplace and the sense of mastery*, Institute of Behavioral Science, University of Colorado at Boulder, November.
[62] Ibid.
[63] Bureau of Labor Statistics. 2001. BLS Strategic Plan, October 16, http://www.bls.gov/bls/blsplan02.htm.
[64] *Business Week*. 2003. Waking Up From the American Dream, December 1.
[65] The Mackinac Center for Public Policy. 1999. *Michigan labor law: What every citizen should know*, August.
[66] Ian, J. 2000. Ian's mind jog, *Technology & Learning*, Feb 20, 7, p72.
[67] Ibid.
[68] *Career World*. 2003. Sep 32, 1, p2.
[69] Hobbes' Internet Timeline, http://www.zakon.org/robert/internet/timeline/
[70] Carnall, C. 2001. Learning as an equal partnership: Tutoring [Electronic version]. *The Financial Times*, March 26, 3.
[71] Apollo Group Annual Report. 2001. p. 1.

[72] http://www.astd.org/NR/rdonlyres/6EBE282-1D29-48A7-8A3A357649BB6DB6/0/SOIR_2003_Executive_Summary.pdf.
[73] Ibid.
[74] Meister, J. 2003. Innovative corporate/university alliances, *Chief Learning Officer*, December.
[75] Ibid.
[76] Minter, R. 2003. Trends in higher education, *Fort Worth Business Press*, October 31-November 6, 2003.
[77] Meister, J. 2003. Innovative corporate/university alliances, *Chief Learning Officer*, December.
[78] American Association of Community Colleges. 2000. http://www.aacc.nche.edu/Content/NavigationMenu/AboutCommunityColleges/Fast_Facts1/Fast_Facts.htm.
[79] SallieMae. 2003. *Fall enrollment rates 4-year vs. 2-year institutions*, Chart II.7.
[80] Klor de Alva, J. 2003. Chairman & CEO, Apollo International, Inc., presentation at the NGA Meeting, San Francisco, CA, September 15.
[81] Ibid.
[82] Berry, J. 2003. *The Washington Post*, November 29.
[83] Bureau of Labor Statistics, Non-Farm Employment & U.S. Census Bureau, Per Capita Income.
[84] *Business Week*. 2003. September 29.
[85] Vilsack, T., Governor of Iowa. 2004. Democratic response to President's weekly radio address, February 16.
[86] Bureau of Labor Statistics. 2000. *2001-2003 Winter Occupational Employment Outlook Quarterly*.
[87] National Center for Education Statistics. 1999. http://nces.ed.gov.
[88] American Association of Community Colleges. 2003. http://www.aacc.nche.edu/Content/Navigation/Menu/AboutCommunityColleges/Fast_Facts1/Fast_Facts.htm.
[89] Center for Workforce Preparation. 2003. Market-Responsive Community Colleges Regional Dialogue, September 30, Chicago, IL.
[90] *Orlando Sentinel*. 2003. September 18.
[91] American Association of Community Colleges, Fact Sheet, May 2005.
[92] Ibid.
[93] U.S. Census. 2000. http://www.census.gov/population/projections/nation/detail/d2001_10.pdf.

[94] Eisenberg. 2002. *Toward a national workforce education and training policy,* NCEE Report.
[95] Sum, A., & Harrington, P. 2003. *The hidden crisis in the high school dropout*, Center for Labor Market Studies, Northeastern University, February.
[96] Ibid.
[97] Thompson, T. 2003. Calling the shots, *Northwest Airlines World Traveler*, November.
[98] Palmisano, S. 2003. How the U.S. Can Keep Its Innovation Edge, *Business Week*, November 17.
[99] Garten, J. 2003. Will All Those Jobs Ever Come Back?, *Business Week*, October 6.
[100] Greenspan, A. 2003. Remarks before the World Affairs Council of Greater Dallas, December 11.
[101] Bureau of Economic Analysis, U.S. Department of Commerce.
[102] Ibid.
[103] U.S. Patent and Trademark Office.
[104] *Business Week*. 2004. January 19.
[105] Bureau of Labor Statistics, 2004.